PRACTICING BASIC
SPIRITUAL DISCIPLINES

CHARLES
STANLEY

OLIVER
NELSON™

THOMAS NELSON PUBLISHERS
Nashville

ISBN 0-7852-7294-1

Printed in the United States of America

01 02 03 04 05 PHX 6 5 4 3 2

CONTENTS

THE STRENGTH OF THE BELIEVER

Of one thing we can be certain today—the Lord intends for our faith as Christians to be "rock-solid." At no time do we find the Lord calling His people to be weak in spiritual power, wavering in purpose, or wandering aimlessly through life. We are called, rather, to be strong in faith, certain of our salvation, and sure of our direction and eternal destiny.

One of the Bible's descriptions for the Lord is that of a rock. The psalmist David said this in a praise song to the Lord:

> I will love You, O LORD, my strength.
> The LORD is my rock and my fortress and
> my deliverer;
> My God, my strength, in whom I will trust. (Ps. 18:1–2)

Elsewhere in the psalms, David referred to the Lord as the rock of his strength, the rock of his salvation, and the rock of his refuge (Ps. 62:7; 89:26; 94:22). The Lord was his sure foundation, an immovable, impenetrable fortress.

In the New Testament, we find Jesus referred to as our spiritual Rock (1 Cor. 10:4). He is the chief cornerstone on which the entire church has been built (Eph. 2:20).

When we put our faith in God and trust Jesus Christ to be our Savior and Lord, we are placing ourselves on the sure, firm foundation that never falters and never fails. We are placing ourselves on a foundation that does not shift, crumble, or crack. We are placing ourselves on a foundation that is eternal and unchanging.

As part of God's holy and living temple—a "dwelling place of God in the Spirit"—we are to bear the same qualities as the foundation on which we are built (see Eph. 2:21–22). We are to remain strong in times of crisis or persecution, solid in our understanding of the Scriptures, sure of our relationship with the Lord, and steadfast in our pursuit of all that the Holy Spirit calls us to be and to do. God's people are to be like boulders in a world of shifting sands.

When the world says that black is white and white is black . . . morals don't matter . . . and all things are relative—we are to stand strong as Christians, clearly discerning right from wrong, good from bad, and the eternal from the temporary.

When the world calls us to do what "feels good" and justifies behavior under the banner of "everybody is doing it," we are to stand strong as Christians and declare that our behavior is rooted in our faith, not our emotions, and that even if everybody around us bows to the false gods of this age, we will not bow.

When the world calls us to reject God's commandments as "old-fashioned" or "out of touch," we are to stand strong as Christians and declare that God changes not, His commandments are as applicable today as they were in Bible times, and that God is *always* in touch with the human heart and human need.

When the world calls us to do what is politically "correct," economically expedient, or morally compromising, we are to stand strong as Christians and declare that we choose to be God's people, generous in the help we offer to the needy but pure in our hearts and uncompromising in our belief that God is sovereign and that a holy God requires and desires a holy people.

The Prerequisites for Godly Strength

Any athlete knows that to become strong, he must do certain things. He must eat foods that build up the body physically, he must exercise in ways that produce strength, flexibility, and endurance, and he must get sufficient rest for renewal of his muscles. There is a *discipline* required of those who desire to become good athletes. The greater the person's desire for greatness, the greater the discipline required.

The same is true for us in our spiritual walk. If we truly are going to be strong in the faith, we must follow a spiritual discipline.

We must take into our lives those things that produce strength in us, and eliminate those things that result in weakness, laziness, or spiritual compromise.

We must exercise our spiritual "muscles"—using our faith in ways that promote the spread of the gospel, strengthen the body of Christ, and meet both the physical and spiritual needs we encounter.

We must learn to "rest" in the Lord—trusting Him always to provide for us and protect us against the enemy of our souls.

The Christian life is not a life lived on a whim, following fad beliefs. It is to be a life of consistent, daily discipline. The apostle Paul challenged the Philippians, "Let your conduct be worthy of the gospel of Christ" (Phil. 1:27). That is our goal always.

A Life of Consistency

As a pastor, I have asked countless people, "How are you doing?" and I have received these replies:

"Oh, I'm having my ups and downs."

"Well, I'm going through a wilderness time right now."

"I'm trying to stay on top of things."

Some have admitted to me:

"I'm not as close to the Lord as I should be."

"I've been away from the Lord but I'm on my way back."

"I'm dry right now."

All of these statements say to me that most Christians do not live the *consistently strong* spiritual life that they desire, and which they know God desires for them to live. They are riding the roller coaster of life, rather than walking a steady, upward path.

When I have asked, "What are you doing to be strong spiritually?" I get a variety of answers, but in many cases, I get a response that means, "I don't know what to do." Many haven't even thought it is possible to live a *consistently strong* spiritual life. They take ups and downs for granted, and even expect them.

That is not what the Lord desires for us. Paul said to the Colossians, "I am with you in spirit, rejoicing to see your good order and the steadfastness of your faith in Christ. As you therefore have received Christ Jesus the Lord, so walk in Him, rooted and built up in Him and established in the faith, as you have been taught, abounding in it with thanksgiving" (Col. 2:5–7). He assured the Colossians that they would be "holy, and blameless, and above reproach" if they would "continue in the faith, grounded and steadfast, and [not be] moved away from the hope of the gospel" (Col. 1:22–23).

Paul wrote to the Ephesians, "Be strong in the Lord and in the power of His might" (Eph. 6:10).

What must we do to be strong and to remain strong in spirit?

How are we to discipline our lives to be consistent and unwavering in our walk of faith?

The elements of our disciplined life in Christ are the subject of this Bible study. As you read through these lessons, let me encourage you on these three points:

First, the foundation for our spiritual discipline is the same whether we are newborn babes in Christ—the newly saved—or longtime Christians. We never outgrow our need for the "basics" of spiritual discipline. We never outgrow our need for God's Word, our need to pray, God's command to give, our need for Christian fellowship, or God's call to ministry. No person is so spiritually "mature" that he or she can ignore the basics and remain strong over time.

Second, the foundation for our spiritual discipline is the same regardless of our personal differences. Pastors and laymen need to pursue the same basic spiritual disciplines to be strong in the Lord. Men and women, rich and poor, young and old, highly educated and uneducated . . . all need the same basic spiritual discipline.

Third, the spiritual discipline we are called to pursue in God's Word is one that we each can pursue. I once met a person who said to me, "I'm just not as spiritual as some people. I struggle more." The fact is, we all struggle to remain consistent in our spiritual lives. The fact is also this: God has given each of us both the will necessary to pursue a disciplined spiritual life, and the power of the Holy Spirit to help us remain strong and consistent in our spiritual walk. Our will plus the Holy Spirit's power is true *willpower*. Every person *can* become spiritually disciplined.

As you begin this study today ask yourself these questions:

- *Would I classify myself as a weak or a strong Christian?*

  _____

  _____

- *Am I as consistent in my spiritual life as I desire to be?*

  _____

  _____

- *What am I doing with regularity in order to remain spiritually strong consistently?*

  _____

  _____

LESSON 1

OUR BLUEPRINT FOR STRENGTH

Every building begins with a blueprint. If the engineering is faulty on the blueprint, the structure will be weak in reality.

The same is true for our spiritual life. The strength of our spiritual life rests first and foremost on the absolute, utter reliability and truth of God's Word. Thank God we have a blueprint for spiritual strength that does not fail! The Bible is a blueprint on which we can rely with absolute confidence.

This book is for Bible study. It is not a stand-alone manual. I hope that you will refer to your Bible again and again, and that you will feel free to mark specific words, underline phrases, or write in the margins of your personal Bible.

The Bible not only gives us God's truth, but it also tells us how to apply God's truth to our daily lives. It is a book of genuine wisdom about how to become strong and stay strong spiritually. It is the reference to which we must return continually to make certain that we are staying "on track" in our spiritual growth.

Just as builders return to blueprints often during the construction of a structure, so we must return to the Bible *often* during the development of our personal spiritual lives and the spiritual growth of our church.

Keys to Study

You will be asked in this book to identify with the concepts and verses that are presented by answering one or more of these questions:

- What new insight have you gained?
- Have you ever had a similar experience?
- How do you feel about what you have read?
- In what way are you challenged to act?

Insights

A spiritual insight is something that produces a new degree of understanding. It lies beyond the literal understanding of a fact or an idea and moves a person into a deeper level of *meaning*. Many times we read a particular passage of the Bible and think we know it well, and then God surprises us. Suddenly He reveals new meaning. That is a spiritual insight.

Insights are usually very personal. Most of them involve a way in which the passage applies to something you personally have experienced or are experiencing. Spiritual insights are the direct work of the Holy Spirit in our lives. They are a part of His function as the Spirit of truth. They are very important to us as we seek to grow spiritually and remain spiritually strong.

Ask the Holy Spirit to give you insights every time you open your Bible to read and study it. I believe that's one prayer God delights in answering with a resounding *Yes!* In fact, if you haven't gained new spiritual insights after reading several passages from God's Word, you probably haven't been engaged in the process of genuine study. The person who truly studies God's Word with an open heart and has an eagerness to hear from the Holy Spirit is going to have spiritual insights on a regular basis.

As you receive spiritual insights, make notes about them. The benefit to you lies in the future. When you look back at the margins of your Bible and read what God has shown you or spoken to your heart in the past, and then reflect on how that insight has manifested itself in the subsequent months or years of your life, your faith will grow. I believe it is always a good idea to add a date to a spiritual-insight note you make.

Experiences

Each of us comes to God's Word with a different background in reading and studying the Bible and with a different level of understanding about the Bible's contents. We also come to God's Word with a unique set of personal experiences, cultural experiences, and language ability. Therefore, each of us has a slightly different perspective on any Scripture reading. In a group setting, these differences can sometimes create problems. Those with a long history of regularly reading God's Word may lose patience with those who are just beginning to study the Bible, and beginners may feel overwhelmed or lost, although neither is necessarily true for all groups.

What we do have in common are *life* experiences. We each can point to times in which we have found the truth of a Bible passage to be highly relevant or meaningful to our lives. We can recall times when the Bible encouraged, convicted, challenged, or directed us in some way. We have experiences about which we can say, "I know that truth in the Bible is real because of what happened to me," or "That passage speaks to me because it is directly related to an experience I am having."

Our experiences do not make the Bible true. The Bible is truth, period. As we share experiences related to God's Word, however, we discover how far-reaching and amazing the Bible really is. God's Word applies to human life in more ways than we ever thought! When we share our Bible-related experiences, we see how God's Word speaks to every person, to every aspect of human nature, and to every human condition or problem.

Sharing experiences is important for your spiritual growth. Not only do you benefit from hearing the experiences of others, but you also benefit from sharing your own experiences. Your ability to verbalize what you believe is strengthened, and in the process, your abilities to witness, teach, and counsel are enhanced.

Our tendency when sharing experiences is to judge the experience of another person in the light of our own experience. A judgmental attitude—especially toward a person's spiritual discipline or spiritual growth—can do great harm to another person, as well as cause great friction within a group. Listen. Discuss. Talk about what the Scriptures say and mean to you. But be very careful not to judge or to condemn others for their spiritual immaturity or difficulties in maintaining spiritual discipline.

Emotional Response

Just as we each have different life experiences, so we each have our own emotional responses to God's Word. No emotional response is more valid than another. One person may be frightened by the message of a particular verse or passage even as another person feels great joy or relief at reading the same words. Face your emotions honestly, and allow others the freedom to share their emotions fully.

Our emotions do not give validity to the Scriptures any more than our experiences do. Emotions should never be trusted as a gauge of faith. Our faith is always to be based on what God says, not on what we feel. The Scriptures are true regardless of the emotions they evoke in us. At the same time, we are wise to recognize that the Bible has an emotional impact on us. We cannot read the Bible with an open heart and mind and not *feel* a particular way. Our emotions are usually related to the way we feel about God, Jesus, the Holy Spirit, the church as a whole, and specific people who may come to mind as we read.

Some people allow themselves to be more vulnerable emotionally than others. Their responses to particular Scripture passages may produce tears or feelings of great elation, longing, or conviction. Allow for the expression of these emotions without judgment in your group setting. Others are more reserved emotionally. This does not mean that they are resistant to God or to the impact of the Bible on their lives. Allow them, also, to "be themselves" emotionally.

Ask yourself why you feel certain emotions. If you feel resistance or fear in your heart, ask yourself why. If you feel sorrow or have a feeling of failure, ask why. Seek answers. Your search for answers can begin a healing or growing process in your spirit.

Bible study groups sometimes get sidetracked by opinions or personal "formulas" for spiritual growth. This can lead quickly to debate, distrust, and confusion. Focus your group sharing on feelings and experiences, not opinions. Scholarly commentaries certainly have their place in teaching us the background of specific passages. But a person's knowledge and opinion actually have little impact on other people within the context of group Bible study. What God says to us individually and directly is what we find to be truly significant. And God often speaks to us in the language of the heart—the silent language of our intuition, emotions, innermost desires, and unvoiced longings. When we share feelings with one another, we grow closer together. Genuine Christian fellowship and friendship have an opportunity to develop. When we share only opinions, we often fail to find the unity of spirit in Christ Jesus that is deeply satisfying and meaningful to the heart.

Challenges

As we read the Bible, we often come to a passage or insight that seems to speak directly to us. Something challenges us to change an aspect of our lives, to feel chastened and say, "I need to do something about that."

We may feel a conviction about sin. We may feel a need to correct something in the way we think or the way we act toward others. We may feel a clear call to do something new— to acquire a new habit or start a new ministry. In my life God never ceases to challenge me just beyond my ability so that I must always rely upon Him to work in me and through me.

God is never content with the status quo. He always wants us to grow to be more like His Son, Jesus Christ, both individually and as churches. As I read the Scriptures and pray, or talk about the Scriptures with other people, I often feel those challenges to grow. I believe it is vitally important, therefore, for us to be aware of the many ways in which God speaks to us through His Word to challenge us, stretch us, change us, and strengthen us.

God's ultimate reason for us to know His Word is that we might share His Word with others—through both our actions and words. God not only expects us to know and believe His Word, but to *do* His Word—to keep His commandments, to be His witnesses, to carry on His mission in the world, and to act in the specific ways that He directs us to act (James 1:22).

In the area of spiritual discipline, we can expect God to challenge us to grow and mature spiritually. God expects us to become more like Jesus Christ and to be spiritually vibrant and strong. He longs for us to "grow up" spiritually so that we might experience more and more of Him and experience more and more of His rewards and blessings. My full expectation is that as you engage in this study, God will speak to you about His desires for you, especially His desire to have an ever-deepening relationship with you. Be open to His wooing, His commanding, and His challenges.

Personal or Group Study?

Although you certainly may use this book for a personal Bible study, this book has been designed for group study. If you don't have somebody with whom you can share your insights, experiences, emotions, and challenges, I encourage you to find someone with whom you can share the fruit of what you learn and experience as a result. You may be able to share with a spouse, child, or close friend some of the insights you have into the Scriptures or about spiritual disciplines. Consider starting a Bible study in your home, using this book as the focal point. Perhaps you can talk to your pastor about organizing a Bible study group in your church. There is much to be learned on your own. There is much *more* to be learned as you become part of a small group that desires to grow in the Lord. Be an encouragement to others in their spiritual growth.

Keep the Bible Central

One tendency of a group devoted to the study of spiritual discipline is for the group to become a sharing-techniques group rather than a true Bible study group. Keep the Bible at the center of all you do. Gather around God's Word as if you are gathering around a banquet table for a spiritually nutritious meal.

Prayer

As you begin your Bible study, ask God to give you spiritual eyes to see what He wants you to see in the Scriptures and spiritual ears to hear what He wants you to hear from others in your group. Ask Him to give you new insights, to recall to your memory experiences that relate to what you read, and to help you identify clearly your emotional responses to His Word. Ask Him to reveal to you what He desires for you to be, say, and do. Look for the "next steps" He challenges you to take in your spiritual walk.

As you conclude your study time, ask the Lord to seal what you have learned in your heart so you will never forget it. Ask Him to transform you more into the likeness of Jesus Christ as you meditate on what you have studied. And above all, ask Him to give you the courage to become, say, and do what He has challenged you to become, say, and do.

As we discussed in the introduction, open yourself up as you pray—individually and as a group—to ways in which you might become stronger spiritually. Be keenly aware that God desires for you to grow. Listen closely to the ways in which the Holy Spirit directs your life each day. God desires to speak to your heart during and after your study time about how to experience more of His presence moment by moment, hour by hour, day by day.

Consider these questions:

• *What new insights into spiritual discipline do you hope to gain from this study?*

_____

_____

- *In what areas have you struggled to remain consistently strong in your faith walk?*

  _____

  _____

- *How do you feel about spiritual discipline?*

  _____

  _____

- *In what ways are you feeling challenged to grow stronger spiritually and to become more mature in Christ Jesus?*

  _____

  _____

LESSON 2

OBEDIENCE TO GOD'S COMMANDMENTS

*O*bedience is not a popular word in today's culture. To the world at large, a person will be much more readily accepted if he or she is tolerant, compromising, lenient, or "relational"—seeing all things as relevant and doing one's best to keep everybody happy and satisfied.

God's Word, however, calls us to obedience and specifically, to be obedient to all of God's laws, statutes, and commandments. There can be no spiritual growth—no genuine spiritual power or effective ministry to the lost—without obedience. A rebellious heart is contrary to spiritual strength.

Rebellion is the foremost reason for a *lack* of spiritual authority, a *lack* of intimacy with God, and a *lack* of genuine blessings and rewards from God's hand.

When many of us think of rebels we think of juvenile delinquents, criminals, or those who are opposed to the "establishment" or the current political order. The Bible defines *rebellion* in a much different way—it refers to *any* person who seeks to enact his own set of standards or to "do his own thing" contrary to the commandments of God. Those who willfully choose their way over God's way are rebels.

- *In what ways have you struggled with rebellion—choosing your way over God's way—in the past?*

_____

_____

What the Word Says	**What the Word Says to Me**
God sets the solitary in families; He brings out those who are bound into prosperity; But the rebellious dwell in a dry land. (Ps. 68:6)	
"Woe to the rebellious children," says the LORD, "Who take counsel, but not of Me, And who devise plans, but not of My Spirit, That they may add sin to sin." (Isa. 30:1)	
For rebellion is as the sin of witchcraft, And stubbornness is as iniquity and idolatry. (1 Sam. 15:23)	
Thus says the LORD God of Israel: "Cursed is the man who does not obey the words of this covenant which I commanded your fathers	

in the day I brought them out of
the land of Egypt, from the iron
furnace, saying, 'Obey My voice,
and do according to all that I
command you; so shall you be
My people, and I will be your
God,' that I may establish the
oath which I have sworn to your
fathers, to give them 'a land flow-
ing with milk and honey,' as it is
this day." (Jer. 11:3–5)

- *How do you feel as you read these verses?*

- *In what ways are you feeling challenged in your spirit?*

As much as the Lord stands against rebellion, He supports
and upholds those who are obedient. Obedience to God's
commandments is highly praised by God in the Bible. It is
"better than sacrifice" in His eyes!

What the Word Says

"If you are willing and obedient,
You shall eat the good of the land;
But if you refuse and rebel,
You shall be devoured by the
sword";
For the mouth of the LORD has
spoken. (Isa. 1:19–20)

What the Word Says to Me

mate relationship with God. And having such a relationship with God is what spiritual discipline is all about! The very goal of all spiritual disciplines is to know God more intimately and to experience more of Him at work in us and through us.

• *Do you know anyone who has tried to engineer his or her salvation apart from the shed blood of Jesus Christ? What were the results?*

_____

_____

The Hindrance of Sin

Sin—which might be considered another word for acts of willful disobedience—always has negative consequences. Ultimately, a state of sinfulness brings about a person's spiritual death (Rom. 6:23). But even in the life of the believer who has truly turned to the Lord and received His forgiveness, sin exists and has consequences. It is a tremendous hindrance to the work that the Lord desires to do.

The writer to the Hebrews said,

Therefore we also, since we are surrounded by so great a cloud of witnesses, let us lay aside every weight, and the sin which so easily ensnares us, and let us run with endurance the race that is set before us. (12:1)

Sin is a weight and a snare. It slows us down, trips us up, and at times delays or detours us from fulfilling God's purposes and plans. Part of our obedience to the Lord is to ask the Lord to forgive us *daily* for those things we have thought, said, or done that are contrary to His commandments. That is the only way we can avoid chastening from the Lord. It is the only way we can experience the fullness of God's blessings.

What the Word Says	What the Word Says to Me
For though we walk in the flesh, we do not war according to the flesh. For the weapons of our warfare are not carnal but mighty in God for pulling down strongholds, casting down arguments and every high thing that exalts itself against the knowledge of God, bringing every thought into captivity to the obedience of Christ, and being ready to punish all disobedience when your obedience is fulfilled. (2 Cor. 10:3–6)	....

A Passion to Obey

There are several benchmarks by which we can evaluate if we are obeying God and developing spiritual discipline:

1. Obedience As Our Bottom Line

Obedience to God must become the bottom line of every decision we make. The obedient person sifts every decision through the will of God, asking, "Can I do this and be obedient to God and His commandments and plan for my life?" Even in those situations in which we feel inadequate and find ourselves struggling with fear, suffering, loss, or painful consequences, our desire must be to obey God's will.

• *Recall an experience in which you weighed a decision by sifting it through "the will of God."*

_____

_____

2. Instant Obedience

When the Holy Spirit speaks to an obedient person's heart, that person doesn't even stop to consider whether he will act. He responds instantly.

• *Have you had an experience in which the Holy Spirit prompted you to act in a specific way? Did you obey or disregard the prompting of the Holy Spirit? What were the consequences?*

_____

_____

3. A Yearning for the Heart and Mind of God

The obedient Christian desires to learn more and more about how God works and what God desires. He has a deep yearning to seek the mind of God and to know God better. We certainly will never learn all there is to know about God—we will never know Him with total intimacy. But our desire must be to know Him better and better. For us to grow spiritually, we must ask continually, "What is it that God truly desires for my life? How does God want me to act? What does He want me to say?"

Our role is not to take our plans to God and ask Him to bless them. No! Our role is to ask God what He desires for us to do in, through, and with our lives—our time, our talents, and our material substance—and then do His bidding.

• *In what ways are you feeling challenged in your spirit?*

_____

_____

4. God's Opinion Is All That Matters

To the truly obedient Christian the opinions of others are never more important than the opinion of God. The obedient person has no concern about whether others may reject or ridicule him—the only acceptance that truly counts is God's acceptance. The obedient person may seek out the counsel of godly people, but he does not act on human consensus. He does what God requires even if all counsel is against God's command.

• *How do you feel when others criticize your obedience to God?*

_____

_____

5. Willing to Accept Consequences of Obedience

The obedient person is willing to accept adverse consequences of his obedience. He is willing to suffer for Christ's sake—not eager to suffer, but joyful in the midst of suffering. As Jesus taught, "Blessed are those who are persecuted for righteousness' sake, for theirs is the kingdom of heaven" (Matt. 5:10).

What the Word Says	What the Word Says to Me
For if we live, we live to the Lord;	_____
and if we die, we die to the Lord.	_____
Therefore, whether we live or die,	_____
we are the Lord's. (Rom. 14:8)	_____
Eli said to Samuel, "Go, lie down;	_____
and it shall be, if He calls you, that	_____
you must say, 'Speak, Lord, for	_____
Your servant hears.'" (1 Sam. 3:9)	_____

He said, "I am Jesus, whom you
are persecuting. But rise and
stand on your feet; for I have
appeared to you for this purpose, to make you a minister
and a witness both of the things
which you have seen and of the
things which I will yet reveal to
you" . . . Therefore, King
Agrippa, I was not disobedient to
the heavenly vision, but declared
first to those in Damascus and in
Jerusalem, and throughout all the
region of Judea, and then to the
Gentiles, that they should repent,
turn to God, and do works befit-
ting repentance. (Acts 26:15–16,
19–20)

The Rewards of Obedience

There are a number of consequences to our being obedient
to God's Word. Not all of them are positive. Every person who
lives in obedience to the Lord will suffer to a certain degree
because he is going against the grain of the world. The positive
rewards from God, however, far outweigh anything the world
might do to the believer:

- *A growing faith.* The obedient person is one who sees
  God's faithfulness in action and grows in faith as a
  result.

- *Blessings.* God bestows His blessings upon those who are obedient, not only spiritual blessings but financial, material, and relational blessings.
- *An enlarged view of God.* The person who is obedient moves into a more intimate relationship with God. The closer we come to God, the more we experience His love and the more we are able to see His omnipotence and omniscience (His infinite and absolute power and wisdom). Those who are obedient grow in reverence for God, and at the same time, have an increased sense of security in God's deep and abiding love.
- *A greater effectiveness in witnessing.* Those who view a person's obedience—family members, friends, coworkers, fellow church members, lost souls—will be impacted by an obedient person's steadfast faithfulness to God's commands. They can't help but be influenced in a positive way toward the gospel, regardless of what they may claim.
- *Greater ability to discern the Holy Spirit at work in our lives.* Those who are obedient hear the Holy Spirit with greater clarity and have greater recognition of His voice. They are more readily able to discern with accuracy what the Holy Spirit directs them to do, and when and how to act.

What the Word Says

Whether it is pleasing or displeasing, we will obey the voice of the LORD our God to whom we send you, that it may be well with us when we obey the voice of the LORD our God. (Jer. 42:6)

What the Word Says to Me

To those who are self-seeking and
do not obey the truth, but obey
unrighteousness—indignation and
wrath, tribulation and anguish, on
every soul of man who does evil, of
the Jew first and also of the Greek;
but glory, honor, and peace to
everyone who works what is good.
(Rom. 2:8–10)

Obedience is truly the "bottom line" for all spiritual discipline. Everything else we *do* that builds spiritual discipline is
established on a foundation of obedience—we pray, for
example, in obedience to God's command to pray. We read
God's Scriptures because we desire to know God's statutes and
obey them, and also because we are commanded to study the
Word. Our quest to know the Lord is rooted in obedience at all
times.

Now, to "obey" is not the ultimate motivation for spiritual
discipline—a love for God, a longing to know God, our faith in
God are the true motives for the mature believer. But obedience is required if we are to grow spiritually and experience
more and more of God's love.

Do you truly desire to be obedient to the Lord's commandments? Do you truly want to put aside every sign and
weight that can keep you from experiencing spiritual power
and strength? Do you truly long to move into greater intimacy
with your heavenly Father?

- *What new insights do you have into the relationship between
obedience and spiritual growth?*

• *In what ways are you feeling challenged in your spirit today?*

_____

_____

LESSON 3

CONFORMATION TO CHRIST

Do you have a spiritual goal today?

Without a goal, we rarely achieve all that we can achieve, or desire to achieve. That is true in the spiritual realm just as much as it is true in the worlds of business and personal finance, family life, education, or physical fitness.

The goal for every Christian is clearly stated by the apostle Paul in his letter to the Romans:

> And we know that all things work together for good to those who love God, to those who are the called according to His purpose. For whom He foreknew, He also predestined to be conformed to the image of His Son, that He might be the firstborn among many brethren. Moreover whom He predestined, these He also called; whom He called, these He also justified; and whom He justified, these He also glorified. (Rom. 8:28–30)

• *What new insights do you have into this passage from Romans?*

_____

_____

The Conformation Process

I want to call your attention specifically to three key truths in this passage from Romans 8:28–30. These are truths that are important for you as you practice basic spiritual disciplines and seek to grow in Christ.

1. Destined to Be Conformed

From the beginning, God has chosen you to be His beloved child and to be conformed to the image of Christ. "To be conformed" implies that, at present, a person is *not* conformed to Christ's image, and we certainly know that to be true for each one of us. None of us have lived a sinless life . . . not one of us is without fault . . . all of us have had imperfect backgrounds and imperfect childhoods and experiences that have left us wounded and scarred . . . all of us need healing in some area of life to be whole. No matter how mature we are in our walk with the Lord, there is *more* that can and must be changed in us for us to be *fully* like Christ Jesus—spiritually, emotionally, and psychologically. Only the Lord can say, "I change not" because only the Lord can say, "I do not need change." Every one of us is in a position to look in the mirror and say as a prayer to the Lord, "Change me in the ways You know I need to be changed."

- *How do you feel about your destiny as a Christian to be conformed to Christ's image?*

———————————————————————————

———————————————————————————

- *How do you feel about the need for change in your life?*

———————————————————————————

———————————————————————————

What the Word Says	**What the Word Says to Me**
Purge me with hyssop, and I shall be clean;	
Wash me, and I shall be whiter than snow . . .	
Hide Your face from my sins,	
And blot out all my iniquities.	
Create in me a clean heart, O God,	
And renew a steadfast spirit within me . . .	
Restore to me the joy of Your salvation,	
And uphold me by Your generous Spirit.	
Then I will teach transgressors Your ways,	
And sinners shall be converted to You. (Ps. 51:7, 9–10, 12–13)	
Put away the evil of your doings from before My eyes.	
Cease to do evil,	
Learn to do good;	
Seek justice,	
Rebuke the oppressor. (Isa. 1:16–17)	

• *In what ways are you feeling challenged in your spirit?*

2. Conformed to Christ's Image

To be conformed to "Christ's image" means that a person is an accurate and total reflection of Christ. In other words, when others look at us, they cannot tell from what we say and do that we are acting in any way *contrary* to what Jesus would have said and done if He were walking this earth in fleshly form today. A person who is *completely* conformed to Christ's image would think, speak, and act in any given situation exactly as Christ would think, speak, and act.

Again, we know this is not true for any person. We all have sinned and continue to sin, even though we have no desire to sin. We are imperfect, finite, fleshly creatures.

Nevertheless, we are *called* by God—challenged by God, compelled by God—to grow in our likeness of Christ until that day when God fully perfects us and we are in the image of Christ Jesus.

What the Word Says	What the Word Says to Me
But we all, with unveiled face, beholding as in a mirror the glory of the Lord, are being transformed into the same image from glory to glory, just as by the Spirit of the Lord. (2 Cor. 3:18)	....
Do not lie to one another, since you have put off the old man with his deeds, and have put on the new man who is renewed in knowledge according to the image of Him who created him, where there is neither Greek nor	....

Jew . . . but Christ is all and in all.
(Col. 3:9–11)

- *How do you feel about being conformed fully to the point where you reflect Christ's own nature?*

3. God's Work, Not Ours

Paul never told the Romans that they were to strive to be perfect or strive to be conformed to Christ. He said that this would be the work of the Holy Spirit in them. Look again at Romans 8:28–30 on the first page of this chapter and circle each *He* that you find in that passage. It is God who does the foreknowing, the predestining, the conforming, the calling, the justifying, and the glorifying. What tremendous relief this should give to those who are struggling today to "get good" so they can "get God." The conforming work in us is not something for which we are totally responsible. We are to do what we know to do—live by faith and obey by our will—and then trust God to do a transforming work in us.

What the Word Says	What the Word Says to Me
For by grace you have been saved through faith, and that not of yourselves; it is the gift of God, not of works, lest anyone should boast. For we are His workmanship, created in Christ Jesus for good works, which God prepared beforehand that we should walk in them. (Eph. 2:8–10)	

For we ourselves were also once foolish, disobedient, deceived, serving various lusts and pleasures, living in malice and envy, hateful and hating one another. But when the kindness and the love of God our Savior toward man appeared, not by works of righteousness which we have done, but according to His mercy He saved us, through the washing of regeneration and renewing of the Holy Spirit, whom He poured out on us abundantly through Jesus Christ our Savior, that having been justified by His grace we should become heirs according to the hope of eternal life. (Titus 3:3–7)

Wash me thoroughly from my iniquity,
And cleanse me from my sin. (Ps. 51:2)

• *How do you feel about the conforming work in our lives being the work of the Lord, and not something we must strive to do in our own strength?*

Our Ultimate Purpose in Life

A Christian should never have a doubt about what he or she is to do in this life—what goals he should set or what pursuits she should follow. Our ultimate goal and purpose in life are to do those things that conform us to Christ's image. Nothing else that we do will have the same eternal reward as the pursuit of Christ.

Developing the Mind of Christ

Most of us have seen the bracelets and bumper stickers that say "WWJD"—What Would Jesus Do. While that is a wonderful message, it is far from complete. We are not only to do what Jesus would *do*, but we are to say what He would say and think and believe what He thinks and believes.

In writing to the Romans, the apostle Paul very specifically taught not only *whom* we are to be conformed to, but also what we are *not* to be conformed to:

And do not be conformed to this world, but be transformed by the renewing of your mind, that you may prove what is that good and acceptable and perfect will of God. (Rom. 12:2)

To have the mind of Christ is to

• *Have a desire to serve others.* The person who thinks as Jesus thinks has an automatic impulse to help others in need. He doesn't even stop to think about whether he should help a person who is in trouble, sorrow, or sickness. He moves immediately to that person's side to offer whatever assistance he can give, both practical and spiritual.

- *Have a perfect understanding of right and wrong.* The person who thinks like Jesus is a person who has righteous and pure thoughts. He knows God's absolutes and God's desires for *good.* He doesn't have to contemplate whether an activity, event, behavior, statement, or thought is "right"—he knows immediately whether something lines up with God's commandments and God's nature. He has the ability to discern a lie from the truth, and to know whether a thought is a temptation from the enemy or a directive from the Holy Spirit.
- *Clearly discern spiritual matters.* Because the person who thinks like Jesus is strongly rooted in obedience to God's commandments and knows the nature of God, he is able to discern clearly between false and true doctrines. He is able to judge the biblical authenticity of spiritual manifestations. He knows how to judge the spirits and to determine if something truly is from God.
- *Make wise decisions and choices.* The person who thinks like Jesus knows how to make godly decisions, including how to choose friends and coworkers.

- *In your life, can you look back and see how you have developed the mind of Christ since you were born again? Cite specific ways in which you did not formerly "think" or "speak" or "act" like Jesus . . . but now do.*

_____

_____

What the Word Says

Let this mind be in you which was also in Christ Jesus, who, being in the form of God, did not

What the Word Says to Me

----

consider it robbery to be equal
with God, but made Himself of
no reputation, taking the form of
a bondservant. (Phil. 2:5–7)

Put off, concerning your former
conduct, the old man which grows
corrupt according to the deceitful
lusts, and be renewed in the spirit of
your mind . . . that you put on the
new man which was created according to God, in true righteousness
and holiness. (Eph. 4:22–24)

Gird up the loins of your mind,
be sober, and rest your hope fully
upon the grace that is to be
brought to you at the revelation
of Jesus Christ. (1 Peter 1:13)

There is a God in heaven who
reveals secrets. (Dan. 2:28)

If any of you lacks wisdom, let
him ask of God, who gives to all
liberally and without reproach,
and it will be given to him. But let
him ask in faith, with no doubting. (James 1:5–6)

We do not have the mind of Christ instantly upon our con-
version to Christ. Just as a newborn baby grows in his ability

to understand the world, so the newborn Christian must grow in his understanding of God's nature, God's commandments, and the fullness of God's Word.

Furthermore, the will of a person is always involved. You must *want* to develop the mind of Christ. You must *seek* to know God's Word so that you can find God's answers, direction, and solutions. You must *ask* God to impart to you His wisdom.

Conformation Through Suffering

There is another aspect to our being conformed to Christ that many Christians do not like to face: suffering. The Christian life is not immune to suffering—in fact, in many ways the call of Christ is a call to suffer. It is a call to identify with those who are hurting, which always requires a sacrifice of self and a laying aside of one's pride. The call of Christ is also a call to be willing to experience the persecution of the world and to suffer rejection. We *identify* with Christ in our sufferings, for He, too, suffered and aligned Himself with those who suffered.

For most Christians, the most fertile time of spiritual growth in their lives comes during a time of suffering—of crisis, struggle, illness, persecution, loss, pain, rejection. Suffering is the means God often uses to perfect us and to create in us the true character of the Holy Spirit. I challenge you *not* to shy away from difficult challenges or troublesome people . . . but rather, to see them as opportunities to minister the love of Christ.

* *How do you feel about suffering being an integral part of your conformation to Christ?*

_____

_____

What the Word Says

Blessed be the God and Father of our Lord Jesus Christ, the Father of mercies and God of all comfort, who comforts us in all our tribulation, that we may be able to comfort those who are in any trouble, with the comfort with which we ourselves are comforted by God. For as the sufferings of Christ abound in us, so our consolation also abounds through Christ. (2 Cor. 1:3–4)

Therefore, since Christ suffered for us in the flesh, arm yourselves also with the same mind, for he who has suffered in the flesh has ceased from sin, that he no longer should live the rest of his time in the flesh for the lusts of men, but for the will of God. (1 Peter 4:1–2)

What the Word Says to Me

• *What new insights do you have into the goal of spiritual discipline being a conformation to Christ?*

• *In what ways are you feeling challenged in your spirit?*

LESSON 4

A PERSONAL STUDY OF THE SCRIPTURES

For a person truly to develop the mind of Christ, to move into obedience to God's commandments, and to become more conformed to Christ, a person must *know* God's Word. The person who seeks to experience more of the presence and power of God must discipline himself to read and study God's Word for himself. There is no substitute for it!

Your study of God's Word must be

- *Personal.* I meet people all the time who admit to me that they take their Bible to church and they read along as the pastor reads a passage of Scripture or preaches on it, and then they let their Bible gather dust the rest of the week. Some say, "I listen to teaching tapes about the Bible." Others tell me they read books that are religious or that are about what God says in the Bible. While these are all good things to do, none of them are a substitute for personal reading and study of God's Word.

Why? Because to know God's Word is not only to know the content of God's Word—the stories, the commandments, the teachings. It is to know how to *apply* God's Word to daily life. We each have different jobs, roles, family affiliations, cultural settings, communities, and churches. We have different needs—physical, financial, relational, emotional, and spiritual. We are at different levels of spiritual maturity. We *must* read and study the Bible for ourselves to *allow the Bible to speak to our unique, individual circumstances, situations, and relationships.*

The primary way God is going to speak to you is through His Word. Certainly God can and does speak to people through other means, but His *primary* way of speaking to men and women today is through His Word. As you read His Word, ask the Holy Spirit to open your eyes to understanding and impart to you the specific knowledge that *you* need directly from God.

- *Can you recall an instance in which the Lord spoke something very specifically to you from His Word?*

  _____

  _____

- *Daily.* For you continually to grow in the Lord and to remain strong in the Lord, you must read God's Word daily. Why read the Bible daily? Because our lives are lived daily. A part of the Lord's Prayer is, "Give us this day our daily bread" (Matt. 6:11). "Bread" refers not only to physical bread, but also to the spiritual bread we need to feed our souls.

No person eats only once a week; we all eat daily, usually several times a day. What is true for the physical is also true for the spiritual. We need to read the Bible daily to give our minds and hearts the spiritual nutrition they need to face life's daily demands.

Just as we wash our bodies daily, so we must wash our minds daily in God's Word. The Word of God has a cleansing action on us. It convicts us of our daily sins—both things we have done and things we should have done—so that we might confess our sins daily and live in a constant state of repentance.

What the Word Says	What the Word Says to Me
Christ also loved the church and gave Himself for her, that He might sanctify and cleanse her with the washing of water by the word, that He might present her to Himself a glorious church, not having spot or wrinkle or any such thing, but that she should be holy and without blemish. (Eph. 5:25–27)	
Blessed are the undefiled in the way, Who walk in the law of the LORD! Blessed are those who keep His testimonies, Who seek Him with the whole heart! They also do no iniquity; They walk in His ways. You have commanded us To keep Your precepts diligently.	

Oh, that my ways were directed   ....
To keep Your statutes!   ....
Then I would not be ashamed, ...
When I look into all Your   ....
commandments. (Ps. 119:1–6)   ....

- *Understandable.* Read a Bible version that you understand.
  There is no benefit to you in reading a version that seems
  like a foreign language to you. And then, as you read your
  Bible every day, read it until you gain meaning and
  understanding. Don't let your mind wander to other things;
  concentrate on what you are reading. Don't just read the
  words at the surface. Look for the deeper meaning in the
  passage. Ask yourself continually, "How does this apply to
  what I am facing right now? What is God really saying to me?
  What is the deeper meaning of this verse? Why is this passage
  important for me not only to read, but also to remember?"

As you read your Bible daily, look for connections between
what you are reading and what you have read previously. Look
at the broader context of a passage—most passages of Scripture
are directly connected to those passages immediately preceding
it and immediately following it. Also look for the ways in which
a passage might be linked to other passages on the same general
theme, both in the Old Testament and New Testament. Look
for links between what Jesus said and what Paul taught, John
taught, or Peter taught. Look for ways in which Jesus fulfills the
teachings of the Old Testament. Look for symbols and key
words that are repeated again and again, from cover to cover.
The more you make connections between what you read in one
place in the Bible with other references, the more you will grow
in your understanding of the *whole* of God's Word.

What the Word Says	**What the Word Says to Me**
Whom will he teach knowledge? And whom will he make to understand the message? . . . For precept must be upon precept, precept upon precept, Line upon line, line upon line, Here a little, there a little. (Isa. 28:9–10)	....
Through Your precepts I get understanding; Therefore I hate every false way. Your word is a lamp to my feet And a light to my path. (Ps. 119:104–5)	....

- *Prayerful.* As you read the Bible, ask the Holy Spirit to reveal Christ to you. Ask the Holy Spirit to show you how He desires for you to live. Ask Him to reveal to you specific guidance for the decisions you are currently facing. Ask the Holy Spirit to show you how to apply what you read to your life.

What the Word Says	**What the Word Says to Me**
I will meditate on Your precepts, And contemplate Your ways. I will delight myself in Your statutes; I will not forget Your word. Deal bountifully with Your servant,	....

That I may live and keep Your
word.
Open my eyes, that I may see
Wondrous things from Your law.
(Ps. 119:15–18)

You are good, and do good;
Teach me Your statutes. (Ps.
119:68)

The Benefits of Reading the Bible

The more you read your Bible, the greater your understanding will be about God's commandments and God's goals
for your life. You will see more clearly *how* the Lord desires for
you to live. Very specifically, you are going to gain a new or
deeper understanding about the call of God on your life in these
four areas:

1. A Godly Life

We each are called to live godly lives—holy, pure, and
righteous. Again and again, we find stories in the Bible that
might be described as "before" and "after" spiritual makeovers.
Again and again, we find God's directives to "put off" our old
nature and "put on" the character of Christ Jesus. The more
you read your Bible, the more you are going to come face-to-face
with practical changes that God desires for you to make in the
way you think, speak, and act.

Consider this very applicable passage from Ephesians:

Therefore, putting away lying, "Let each one of you speak
truth with his neighbor," for we are members of one another.

"Be angry, and do not sin": do not let the sun go down on your wrath, nor give place to the devil. Let him who stole steal no longer, but rather let him labor, working with his hands what is good, that he may have something to give him who has need. Let no corrupt word proceed out of your mouth, but what is good for necessary edification, that it may impart grace to the hearers . . . Let all bitterness, wrath, anger, clamor, and evil speaking be put away from you, with all malice. And be kind to one another, tenderhearted, forgiving one another, even as God in Christ forgave you. (Eph. 4:25–29, 31–32)

In just a few verses, the apostle Paul gave several specific instructions about what it means to live a godly life. There can be little room for misinterpretation of these verses! God's Word continually challenges us to live exemplary, sinless lives. Not only does the Lord desire for us to live genuinely *good,* righteous lives—but He also makes it possible for us to live such lives by the power of His Holy Spirit.

• *In what ways are you feeling challenged in your spirit by the Word of God after reading the above verses from Ephesians 4?*

_____

_____

What the Word Says	What the Word Says to Me
Your word I have hidden in my heart, That I might not sin against You. (Ps. 119:11)	
Therefore do not be unwise, but understand what the will of the Lord is. (Eph. 5:17)	

2. Eternal Purpose

We each are called to invest our lives in those things that have eternal purpose. From cover to cover, the Bible speaks of God's everlasting nature, His desire for us to be with Him for all eternity, and His eternal purposes. The more you read your Bible, the more you will gain an eternal perspective and grow in your understanding that only those things that are linked to Christ Jesus truly *last*.

You will also gain an understanding that there is no such thing as a "secular job." All jobs exist so that Christ might be manifested in them and through them. All circumstances and situations exist so that God's love, His healing, and His forgiveness might be made known. No part of your life is apart from Christ—rather, Christ desires to touch every aspect of your life with His *eternal* presence and power. And because of this, your life has tremendous meaning. The greatest satisfaction in life comes in knowing that Christ is *in you*, and that He is accomplishing His eternal purposes not only in you, but through you.

- *How do you feel about the fact that ALL aspects of your life can have meaning in the context of Christ's eternal purposes?*

_____

_____

What the Word Says	What the Word Says to Me
Your testimonies I have taken as a heritage forever,	
For they are the rejoicing of my heart.	
I have inclined my heart to perform Your statutes	
Forever, to the very end. (Ps. 119:111–112)	

3. A Role in God's Plan

We each are called to a specific role as part of God's greater purpose for all mankind. The more you read your Bible, the more you are going to gain a vision for God's greater purposes and plans for mankind. You are going to see yourself in the context of God's greater will. No longer is the big "I" at the center of the universe—rather, Christ is central. You will gain an understanding that God does not exist for *you*, but rather, you exist for *God*. God doesn't exist to be molded into your purpose, but rather, you were created to be part of His purpose. God's purpose for your life is that you might bring glory to Christ Jesus and that, by your witness, the world may come to know Jesus Christ as Savior and Lord.

Jesus challenged His disciples, "Go therefore and make disciples of all the nations, baptizing them in the name of the Father and of the Son and of the Holy Spirit, teaching them to observe all things that I have commanded you; and lo, I am with you always, even to the end of the age" (Matt. 28:19–20).

To "make disciples" is defined by Jesus as both "baptizing" and "teaching." To make disciples, we must be both prepared and *willing* to teach others everything that we learn from God's Word, not necessarily in a formal way, but teaching the truth of God informally in our daily conversations and by being a witness for Christ every time we have an opportunity to share the gospel.

• *What new insights do you have into Matthew 28:19–20?*

_____

_____

4. Victory over Satan

We each are called to have victory over the enemy of our souls. The more we read the Bible, the more we learn *how* to have victory over sin and over the enemy of our souls. We have greater strength to withstand the devil's temptations.

When Jesus was tempted by the devil, He did not respond with human wisdom, but rather, by quoting the Word of God. Read again the account of Jesus' temptations and note how He replied to each of them:

Then Jesus was led up by the Spirit into the wilderness to be tempted by the devil. And when He had fasted forty days and forty nights, afterward He was hungry. Now when the tempter came to Him, he said, "If You are the Son of God, command that these stones become bread."

But He answered and said, "It is written, 'Man shall not live by bread alone, but by every word that proceeds from the mouth of God.'" [see Deut. 8:3]

Then the devil took Him up into the holy city, set Him on the pinnacle of the temple, and said to Him, "If You are the Son of God, throw Yourself down" . . .

Jesus said to him, "It is written again, 'You shall not tempt the LORD your God.'" [see Deut. 6:16]

Again, the devil took Him up on an exceedingly high mountain, and showed Him all the kingdoms of the world and their glory. And he said to Him, "All these things I will give You if You will fall down and worship me."

Then Jesus said to him, "Away with you, Satan! For it is written, 'You shall worship the LORD your God, and Him only you shall serve.'" [see Deut. 6:13]

Then the devil left Him, and behold, angels came and ministered to Him. (Matt. 4:1–11)

To be able to say boldly to the devil, "It is written," a person must first know *what* is written!

What the Word Says	What the Word Says to Me
You, through Your commandments, make me wiser than my enemies. (Ps. 119:98)	....
I have restrained my feet from every evil way, That I may keep Your word. (Ps. 119:101)	....
Deliver me according to Your word. (Ps. 119:170)	....
Take the helmet of salvation, and the sword of the Spirit, which is the word of God. (Eph. 6:17)	....

Bible Study Yields Specific Direction

How do daily Bible reading and Bible study differ? Bible *study* is an intense search of God's Word to learn more about what God has to say on a particular subject. Very often, Bible study is aimed at finding specific answers to specific needs, concerns, questions, or problems.

A person may have questions about why God acts in particular ways. A person may question why God fails to act in a particular situation in the way that we desire or think He should act. A person may have questions about what God wants him to do—which decision or choice he should make, or which path he should follow. These questions should motivate a person to go to his Bible to study what God says on the matter. An honest question is always an excellent beginning point for Bible study!

The apostle Paul wrote to Timothy,

> Be diligent to present yourself approved to God, a worker who does not need to be ashamed, rightly dividing the word of truth. (2 Tim. 2:15)

To "rightly divide" the word of truth means to see the *whole* of God's truth and to separate from the truth anything that might be a lie. It is a sifting process—taking out anything that might pollute or detract from the truth.

Bible study helps us to *refine* our understanding of God's Word. In the refinement of metals such as silver and gold, the metal is heated to an extremely high temperature and is brought to a liquid state. The lighter impurities in the metal float to the top of the liquid and are skimmed off. The heavier and more valuable metal remains at the bottom. That is what happens when we engage in a diligent study of God's Word on a particular matter. We come to an understanding that is clearer, purer, more concentrated. We truly *know* what God has to say on a matter.

- *Have you ever engaged in a study of God's Word that led to a refining of your understanding of God's truth on a particular matter?*

_____

_____

What the Word Says	What the Word Says to Me
Teach me, O LORD, the way of Your statutes,	
And I shall keep it to the end.	
Give me understanding, and I shall keep Your law;	
Indeed, I shall observe it with my whole heart.	
Make me walk in the path of Your commandments,	
For I delight in it.	
Incline my heart to Your testimonies,	
And not to covetousness.	
Turn away my eyes from looking at worthless things,	
And revive me in Your way. (Ps. 119:33–37)	

• *What new insights do you have into the relationship between personal Bible study and greater spiritual strength?*

_____

_____

• *In what ways are you feeling challenged in your spirit?*

_____

_____

GETTING TO KNOW THE LORD

There is only one way to develop a deep friendship and that is to spend time with a person, sharing mutual experiences, each of you communicating as fully as possible your ideas, desires, dreams, hopes, and beliefs. Spending time together, sharing experiences, and talking things over . . . these are the basic ingredients for developing a *relationship*, not only with another human being, but with God.

Are you aware that we are commanded to pray? Jesus said to His disciples, "Watch and pray, lest you enter into temptation. The spirit indeed is willing, but the flesh is weak" (Matt. 26:41). Prayer is not just a good idea, it's God's command. It is a requirement if we are to become and remain strong in the Lord and develop an intimate relationship with Him.

Seven Aspects of an Effective Prayer Life

There are at least seven specific aspects of prayer that we should consider as we seek to become spiritually disciplined and to grow spiritually.

1. Continual Prayer

We are called to *pray continually*. Many Christians pray only in church. Some say a "grace" prayer at mealtimes. Others say bedtime prayers with their children. All of these are appropriate times to pray, but the command to Christians from God's Word is to "pray without ceasing" (1 Thess. 5:17).

How can we pray at all times, without ceasing? By living in an attitude of prayer. To pray is to "communicate with God," which includes both talking to and listening to God. Prayer includes both praise and thanksgiving. To pray without ceasing is to talk to God about virtually everything, and to feel free to do so at any time and in any place. It is to discuss with God any problem or need that you face. It is to praise or thank God immediately when good things come your way. It is to converse with Him about decisions that you must make, circumstances that require your involvement, and issues that you must resolve. It is to be constantly on the alert to see what God desires for you to see, and to have spiritual ears "open" to hear what God desires for you to hear.

- *In your life, how do you "pray without ceasing"?*

_____

_____

Through the centuries, God's people developed a habit of praying "morning, noon, and night." Prayer was not limited to these times, but rather, it was offered as a community at these times every day. I know of no better way to start a day and end a day than in prayer. The greatest way to frame a day is to frame it in prayer—seeking God's guidance, health, protection, and wisdom for the coming day as you pray in the morning, and thanking God for His abundant provision to you as you prepare to sleep in the evening.

I believe God is pleased when you set aside specific times to pray. To do so is to make prayer an intentional part of your life; it is to develop the *habit* of prayer, which is one of the most beneficial habits you can ever develop. It is to say to God, to yourself, and to others, "I value my relationship with God, and I am setting aside a part of every day just to be with Him and to talk things over with Him."

- *In your life, how have you incorporated prayer into your daily schedule?*

_____

_____

What the Word Says

My voice You shall hear in the morning, O LORD;
In the morning I will direct it to You,
And I will look up. (Ps. 5:3)

[The Levites'] duty was to help the sons of Aaron in the service of the house of the LORD . . . to stand every morning to thank and praise the LORD, and likewise at evening. (1 Chron. 23:28, 30)

Let my prayer be set before You as incense,
The lifting up of my hands as the evening sacrifice. (Ps. 141:2)

What the Word Says to Me

_____

_____

_____

_____

_____

_____

_____

_____

_____

_____

_____

_____

_____

_____

The effective, fervent prayer of a
righteous man avails much.
(James 5:16)

2. Petitioning for Our Needs

We are to pray for God to meet our needs, including our
need for forgiveness. It is not self-centered for you to pray for
yourself, your family, or your loved ones. God wants you to pray
for your own needs! The nature of the need may be physical,
material, financial, relational, emotional, or spiritual—no need
is too small or too great to take to God. A part of our prayer
every day should be a prayer confessing our sins and asking
God to forgive us, cleanse us, and to help us make the necessary changes in our lives so that we do not keep repeating sin.

What the Word Says

Is anyone among you suffering?
Let him pray. (James 5:13)

Confess your trespasses to one
another, and pray for one
another, that you may be healed.
(James 5:16)

[The LORD said,] "If My people
who are called by My name will
humble themselves, and pray and
seek My face, and turn from their
wicked ways, then I will hear
from heaven, and will forgive
their sin and heal their land." (2
Chron. 7:14)

What the Word Says to Me

[Jesus taught,] "Give us this day	....
our daily bread.	....
And forgive us our debts,	....
As we forgive our debtors.	....
And do not lead us into tempta-	....
tion,	....
But deliver us from the evil one."	....
(Matt. 6:11–13)	....

3. Praise and Thanksgiving

We are to accompany our petitions with praise and thanksgiving. When Paul urged the early church to pray without ceasing, he said this: "Rejoice always, pray without ceasing, in everything give thanks; for this is the will of God in Christ Jesus for you" (1 Thess. 5:16–18).

First, rejoice. Give praise. Be grateful that you have a relationship with the Lord. Praise Him for His wonderful deeds. Praise Him for all that He is, and all that He has done, including the specific things He has done, is doing, and will do in your life.

Second, make your petitions. Tell God your concerns and needs.

And third, give thanks that God is already working on your behalf to cause *all* things to be for your eternal good (see Rom. 8:28). Our prayers take on a much different tone and character when we begin them with praise and end them with thanksgiving!

When Jesus gave His model prayer to His disciples, He began it with words of praise: "Our Father in heaven, hallowed be Your name" (Matt. 6:9). To "hallow" the Lord's name is to declare it holy and worthy to be lifted higher than any other name. When we say, "Hallowed be Your name," we are praising the name of the Lord, exalting Him to a position of absolute supremacy.

And then look at how the Lord ended His model prayer: "For Yours is the kingdom and the power and the glory forever" (Matt. 6:13). He ended the prayer with praise and thanksgiving. The overall model of the Lord's Prayer is praise, petition, praise.

* *What new insights do you have into the role of praise and thanksgiving in prayer?*

_____

_____

What the Word Says

We give thanks to the God and Father of our Lord Jesus Christ, praying always for you. (Col. 1:3)

Continue earnestly in prayer, being vigilant in it with thanksgiving. (Col. 4:2)

Enter into His gates with thanksgiving,
And into His courts with praise.
Be thankful to Him, and bless His name.
For the LORD is good;
His mercy is everlasting,
And His truth endures to all generations. (Ps. 100:4–5)

What the Word Says to Me

_____

_____

_____

_____

_____

_____

_____

_____

_____

_____

_____

_____

Be anxious for nothing, but in
everything by prayer and supplication, with thanksgiving, let your
requests be made known to God.
(Phil. 4:6)

4. An Attitude of Forgiveness

We are to pray with an attitude of forgiveness toward others. The Bible makes it very clear that unless we forgive others,
we cannot receive God's forgiveness. Our unforgiving attitude
acts as a barrier, keeping us from receiving the fullness of what
God desires to give us. Jesus taught, "If you forgive men their
trespasses, your heavenly Father will also forgive you. But if
you do not forgive men their trespasses, neither will your
Father forgive your trespasses" (Matt. 6:14–15).

What the Word Says

[Jesus taught,] "Judge not, and
you shall not be judged. Condemn
not, and you shall not be con-
demned. Forgive, and you will be
forgiven." (Luke 6:37)

Pray for those who spitefully use
you and persecute you, that you
may be sons of your Father in
heaven. (Matt. 5:44–45)

What the Word Says to Me

5. Praying Without Doubt

We are to pray without doubting and without losing heart.
James said this in his teaching that we are to ask God for wisdom:

"Let him ask in faith, with no doubting, for he who doubts is like a wave of the sea driven and tossed by the wind. For let not that man suppose that he will receive anything from the Lord; he is a double-minded man, unstable in all his ways" (James 1:6–8). This is true not only in our prayers for wisdom, but in *all* our prayers.

Jesus taught, "Assuredly, I say to you, if you have faith and do not doubt . . . also if you say to this mountain, 'Be removed and be cast into the sea,' it will be done. And whatever things you ask in prayer, believing, you will receive" (Matt. 21:21–22).

To pray without doubt and without losing heart is to pray with *faith*. At all times, our prayers must be steeped in faith if they are to be effective.

What the Word Says

I desire therefore that the men pray everywhere, lifting up holy hands, without wrath and doubting. (1 Tim. 2:8)

Then He spoke a parable to them, that men always ought to pray and not lose heart, saying: "There was in a certain city a judge who did not fear God nor regard man. Now there was a widow in that city; and she came to him, saying, 'Get justice for me from my adversary.' And he would not for a while; but afterward he said within himself,

What the Word Says to Me

....

....

....

....

....

....

....

....

....

....

....

....

....

....

'Though I do not fear God nor regard man, yet because this widow troubles me I will avenge her, lest by her continual coming she weary me.'" Then the Lord said, "Hear what the unjust judge said. And shall God not avenge His own elect who cry out day and night to Him, though He bears long with them? I tell you that He will avenge them speedily. Nevertheless, when the Son of Man comes, will He really find faith on the earth?" (Luke 18:1–8)

Take the helmet of salvation, and the sword of the Spirit, which is the word of God; praying always with all prayer and supplication in the Spirit, being watchful to this end with all perseverance and supplication for all the saints. (Eph. 6:17–18)

6. Praying for Our Leaders

We are admonished in God's Word to pray for those in leadership over us. Our prayers should be that those in authority will make decisions that allow us to live in peace and to freely share the gospel. Christians around the world are able to prosper spiritually under all kinds of governments, especially if the leader of the government allows religious freedom and

Practicing Basic Spiritual Disciplines

freedom to share the gospel. Christians are able to work in any kind of environment, even slavery, and prosper spiritually, especially if the "boss" allows expressions of faith and opportunities for time off to worship with other believers.

A prayer for leaders should be a prayer that you and other Christians will be allowed to live in an "environment" that is conducive to godliness and reverence. The apostle Paul taught,

> Therefore I exhort first of all that supplications, prayers, intercessions, and giving of thanks be made for all men, for kings and all who are in authority, that we may lead a quiet and peaceable life in all godliness and reverence. For this is good and acceptable in the sight of God our Savior, who desires all men to be saved and to come to the knowledge of the truth. (1 Tim. 2:1–2)

• *In your life, who are the leaders for whom you pray?*

_____

_____

7. Intercession for Others

We are to ask for the prayers of others and offer prayers for others in need. God desires that we be in a giving and receiving relationship with others, and that as the body of Christ, we mutually bear one another's burdens. The disciples of Jesus were quick to ask for prayer, and to offer prayer for others in need.

After Peter and John had been detained by Jewish authorities for healing a man in the name of Jesus, and then had been released with threats never to speak again in His name, they went immediately to their companions and reported what had happened. The group responded with prayer: "They raised their voice to God with one accord" and prayed, "Lord, look on their threats, and grant to Your servants that with all boldness they may speak Your word, by stretching out Your hand to heal, and that signs and wonders may be done through the name of Your holy Servant Jesus" (Acts 4:24, 29–30). If Peter and John needed and benefited from the prayers of others, how much more so do each one of us need the prayers of fellow believers in Christ Jesus?

If you ever question *what* to pray for another Christian, let me suggest Paul's prayer for the Colossians below. It covers many of the basics that we know with certainty are the will of God for every person.

What the Word Says	What the Word Says to Me
For this reason we . . . do not cease to pray for you, and to ask that you may be filled with the knowledge of His will in all wisdom and spiritual understanding; that you may walk worthy of the Lord, fully pleasing Him, being fruitful in every good work and increasing in the knowledge of God; strengthened with all might, according to His glorious power, for all patience and longsuffering with joy; giving thanks to the Father who has qualified us to be partakers of the inheritance of the saints in the light. (Col. 1:9–12)	

What can the person who prays daily and regularly with faith, perseverance, praise, and thanksgiving—for himself, for those in leadership over him, and for fellow believers—expect?

Answers from God! He can expect God to move obstacles and change situations and bring forth blessings. He can expect to experience a deepening intimacy in his relationship with the Lord. He can expect to grow spiritually and to be strong in faith. God hears our prayers. He answers them for our eternal benefit. And He invites us to an ever-deepening relationship with Him.

• *What new insights do you have into the relationship between prayer and spiritual growth?*

_____

_____

• *In what ways are you feeling challenged in your spirit?*

_____

_____

LESSON 6

LOOKING FOR CHRIST IN ALL THINGS

In the last chapter, we briefly touched upon the fact that listening is an integral part of all communication, including our communication with God. Listening involves far more than simply waiting for God to reply to our prayers. It involves an active listening—an intent watching, waiting, anticipation—for God to speak to us "continually." Listening is to be our attitude toward the Lord always. We are to expect the Lord to speak to us—our hearts and minds open to Him so that He might speak to us "by whatever means" at "whatever time." To listen in this way is to be available to the Lord without hindrance.

Can we develop or train such an attitude? Yes. Our attitudes are mental and emotional habits. Like all other habits, we can practice them and develop them over time. You can *choose* what you will think about and how you will respond to life. The more you make positive, godly choices in your thought life, the more likely those choices are going to be your *habitual responses* in times of crisis or deep need.

Four Ways to Develop
an Attitude of Listening

How can we develop and maintain an attitude of active listening before the Lord? There are four key things we can do to discipline ourselves into developing this habit of listening and of being available to the Lord always:

1. Wait in God's Presence

Set aside times to "wait upon the Lord" in silence. So often we spend our prayer time in talking to the Lord without spending any time just waiting in silence to see what the Lord might say to us. Take time to intentionally sit or kneel in silence before the Lord. Empty your mind of all other thoughts. Concentrate on His Word and His presence with you. Ask Him to speak to you.

Many people today seem to be uncomfortable with silence, especially silence if they are alone. It is in silence, however, that we are able to hear the "still, small voice" of the Lord. Certainly the prophet Elijah knew this. After receiving a death threat from Queen Jezebel, Elijah escaped to an isolated desert area. There, in a cave, he heard the Lord say to him,

> "Go out, and stand on the mountain before the LORD." And behold, the LORD passed by, and a great and strong wind tore into the mountains and broke the rocks in pieces before the LORD, but the LORD was not in the wind; and after the wind an earthquake, but the LORD was not in the earthquake; and after the earthquake a fire, but the LORD was not in the fire; and after the fire a still small voice. So it was, when Elijah heard it, that he wrapped his face in his mantle and went out and stood

in the entrance of the cave. Suddenly a voice came to him, and said, "What are you doing here, Elijah?" (1 Kings 19:11–13)

- *What new insights do you have into this passage from 1 Kings?*

  _____

  _____

- *Have you had an experience in which the Lord spoke to you in such a way that you had no doubt it was the Lord?*

  _____

  _____

What the Word Says	What the Word Says to Me
Wait on the LORD;	....
Be of good courage,	....
And He shall strengthen your heart;	....
Wait, I say, on the LORD! (Ps. 27:14)	....
	....
Rest in the LORD, and wait patiently for Him. (Ps. 37:7)	....
	....
My soul, wait silently for God alone,	....
For my expectation is from Him. (Ps. 62:5)	....
	....
But those who wait on the LORD Shall renew their strength; They shall mount up with wings like eagles,	....

They shall run and not be weary, ...

They shall walk and not faint.   ....

(Isa. 40:31)   ....

2. Practice Frequent Praise

Praise the Lord often, regardless of your circumstances. Many people only praise the Lord when something good happens to them or when they receive an unexpected blessing. The Lord is worthy of our praise at *all* times, in *all* circumstances. We do not praise the Lord on the basis of the circumstance we are in; we praise the Lord on the basis of *who He is* in the midst of the circumstance. We do not praise the Lord because of the way we *feel* but because of *who He is* and the way He feels about us!

Don't limit your praise to the song service at church. Praise the Lord often, in both words and songs that you create spontaneously. All around you, at all times, you can find countless things for which to praise the Lord. Look for those things and voice your praise and thanksgiving to God.

When you are alone in your car . . . alone in an elevator . . . alone in your office or work space . . . alone in your home . . . take that opportunity to voice praise to the Lord for who He is, what He has done through the ages, what He has done in your life and in the lives of your loved ones, and what you know without doubt the Lord is doing for you and will do for you now and throughout all eternity. You can never run out of things for which to praise God.

When you voice praise to the Lord, you open yourself up to experiencing the presence of God with you. The Bible tells us that the Lord is "enthroned" in the praises of His people (Ps. 22:3). The greater your praise, the smaller your problems are likely to appear. The more frequent your praise, the less you will find yourself with time to worry or feel anxious. The more you praise the Lord, the more you are going to "see" things that are worthy of His praise. Your entire attitude will shift from being I-centered and problem-centered, to being God-centered and answer-centered.

- *Have you had experiences in which you felt a renewed presence of the Lord with you as you praised Him?*

_____

_____

- *How do you feel after a time of praising the Lord?*

_____

_____

What the Word Says	What the Word Says to Me
Rejoice in the LORD, O you righteous!	
For praise from the upright is beautiful.	
Praise the LORD with the harp;	
Make melody to Him with an instrument of ten strings.	
Sing to Him a new song;	
Play skillfully with a shout of joy. (Ps. 33:1–3)	
O LORD, You are my God.	
I will exalt You,	
I will praise Your name,	
For You have done wonderful things;	
Your counsels of old are faithfulness and truth. (Isa. 25:1)	

But at midnight Paul and Silas were praying and singing hymns to God, and the prisoners were listening to them. Suddenly there was a great earthquake, so that the foundations of the prison were shaken; and immediately all the doors were opened and everyone's chains were loosed. (Acts 16:25–26)

But you are a chosen generation, a royal priesthood, a holy nation, His own special people, that you may proclaim the praises of Him who called you out of darkness into His marvelous light; who once were not a people but are now the people of God, who had not obtained mercy but now have obtained mercy. (1 Peter 2:9–10)

3. See Christ in All Things

Look for evidence of Christ in every circumstance. In even the worst disaster or most overwhelming crisis, Christ is present. When we find ourselves confused, frustrated, or overwhelmed by situations around us, the best question we can ask is, "Father, what is it that You desire to do in this situation?" Asking that question immediately shifts your focus off the problem and onto the One who has all the answers, solutions, and provision in His hand.

The Lord is utterly faithful, and He is with us *always*. There is no moment of any day of your life that He is beyond hearing your heart's cry or your sincere question. How and when the Lord chooses to speak to you of His purposes is up to the Lord. We cannot force the Lord to answer us *when* we desire an answer, or *in the way* we desire. The person who asks a question of the Lord with a sincere desire for understanding, however, is a person who is going to receive an answer from the Lord in His timing and by His methods. Listen for it!

What the Word Says	What the Word Says to Me
If then you were raised with Christ, seek those things which are above, where Christ is, sitting at the right hand of God. Set your mind on things above, not on things on the earth. (Col. 3:1–2)	
Blessed are those who keep His testimonies, Who seek Him with the whole heart! (Ps. 119:2)	
I love those who love me, And those who seek me diligently will find me. (Prov. 8:17)	
[Jesus said,] "Where two or three are gathered together in My name, I am there in the midst of them." (Matt. 18:20)	

4. Listen for Opportunities to Give a Witness

Look and listen continually for opportunities to witness to Christ. Every conversation you have with a friend or coworker, every encounter you have with a stranger, every chance meeting is a potential opportunity to share a word about God's love. Many people think that to give a witness for the Lord is limited to explaining the plan of salvation. Many times our witness to another person is a reminder of God's love, a word of wisdom from God's Word, or a word of encouragement. Look for ways continually to insert the name of Jesus into your conversations. At times, the Lord may desire for us to admonish or to pray for a person. All of those are ways of witnessing to a person that God cares, God loves, God forgives, and God is present.

Ask the Lord as you prepare to meet with a person who is sick, in need, or just stopping by for a friendly visit, "What would *You* say to this person if You were meeting with him today?" Listen for the Lord's answer.

What the Word Says	What the Word Says to Me
So, as much as is in me, I am ready to preach the gospel to you. (Rom. 1:15)	....
Let them do good, that they be rich in good works, ready to give, willing to share, storing up for themselves a good foundation for the time to come, that they may lay hold on eternal life. (1 Tim. 6:18–19)	....
Sanctify the Lord God in your hearts, and always be ready to give	....

a defense to everyone who asks
you a reason for the hope that is
in you, with meekness and fear;
having a good conscience. (1 Peter
3:15–16)

Eyes to See and Ears to Hear

Jesus frequently called His disciples to have "eyes to see"
and "ears to hear" what God was desiring to do in their midst
(see Matt. 11:15 and 13:9 as examples). Those who had ears
to hear were those who not only heard, but understood, what
the Lord was telling them. That is the goal for all of our listening: a greater understanding about what the Lord is desiring to
communicate to us and through us.

When we spend time listening to the Lord, praise Him frequently, look continually for His presence and work in our
midst, and look continually for opportunities to give witness to
Him, we *are* developing eyes to see and ears to hear.

• *What new insights do you have into the importance of
actively listening and watching for the Lord in your life?*

_____

_____

• *What new insights do you have into the relationship between
actively looking for Christ in all things and your development
of greater spiritual strength?*

_____

_____

• *In what ways are you feeling challenged?*

_____

_____

LESSON 7

FAITHFUL GIVING

The Christian life is intended to be a life of generous giving. One of the most blessed and rewarding aspects of spiritual discipline is giving regularly of one's time, talents, and material substance.

The basic understanding of all genuine believers in Christ Jesus is that everything we have received in this life—every minute we live, every ability we possess, every opportunity we are given, every child we bear, every item of material wealth, and even our abilities to express love and have faith—is a gift to us from God. God gives to us *first*, and it is out of the abundance of His supply to us that we give.

What the Word Says	What the Word Says to Me
All things come from You, and of Your own we have given You. (1 Chron. 29:14)	
And God is able to make all grace abound toward you, that you, always having all sufficiency in all things, may have an abundance	

for every good work. As it is
written:
"He has dispersed abroad,
He has given to the poor;
His righteousness endures forever."
Now may He who supplies seed
to the sower, and bread for food,
supply and multiply the seed you
have sown and increase the fruits
of your righteousness, while you
are enriched in everything for all
liberality, which causes thanksgiving through us to God. (2 Cor.
9:8–11)

Three Attributes of Our Giving

Within the broad understanding that God gives to us first
and is the Source of all we have in life, the Lord challenges us
to three very specific ways of expressing our faith through
giving.

1. Cheerful Giving

We are to be cheerful givers.

Too often, Christians have a negative reaction to those who
preach or teach about giving. In all likelihood, they also have a
negative reaction toward the act of giving! Giving, however, is
commanded by God. Jesus taught, "Give, and it will be given
to you" (Luke 6:38). He said, "Freely you have received, freely
give" (Matt. 10:8). Giving is a means of activating our faith,
meeting needs, and bringing about an abundant return. When

we truly catch a glimpse of the great rewards associated with our giving, we cannot help but be cheerful!

We do not give to God in order to "pay God" for anything. God's gift of salvation to us is a free gift motivated by His unlimited love for us. The same is true for all of God's gifts to us—He gives to us because we are His beloved children.

Rather, our giving to God sets in motion an opportunity for God to meet our needs, meet the needs of others, and cause a great abundance of joy and blessings to come our way. Jesus said that when we give, what is returned to us will be in "good measure, pressed down, shaken together, and running over will be put into your bosom. For with the same measure that you use, it will be measured back to you" (Luke 6:38). God multiplies what we give in ways we cannot understand . . . but in which we surely can receive!

- *How do you feel about giving to God?*

_____

_____

- *In your life, have you experienced the joy and abundance that come from cheerful giving?*

_____

_____

What the Word Says

So let each one give as he purposes in his heart, not grudgingly or of necessity; for God loves a cheerful giver. (2 Cor. 9:7)

You shall seek the place where the LORD your God chooses,

What the Word Says to Me

_____

_____

_____

_____

_____

_____

out of all your tribes, to put His
name for His dwelling place; and
there you shall go. There you
shall take your burnt offerings,
your sacrifices, your tithes, the
heave offerings of your hand,
your vowed offerings, your
freewill offerings, and the first-
born of your herds and flocks.
And there you shall eat before the
LORD your God, and you shall
rejoice in all to which you have
put your hand, you and your
households, in which the LORD
your God has blessed you. (Deut.
12:5–7)

2. Consistent Giving

We are to be consistent givers.

God sets the standard for our giving as a tithe of what we receive—a tithe being one-tenth. Our giving is not to be sporadic or scattered, but rather, consistent and focused. As we receive, we are to give a tenth to God's work—regularly. We are to give to the place where we participate in the worship of the Lord— the tithe is not intended for a "charitable organization" but for a work that bears the Lord's name. It is to further the work of the Lord, which is the spreading of the gospel and the teaching of God's Word.

Read this passage from Malachi:

"Will a man rob God?
Yet you have robbed Me!

But you say,
'In what way have we robbed You?'
In tithes and offerings.
You are cursed with a curse,
For you have robbed Me,
Even this whole nation.
Bring all the tithes into the storehouse,
That there may be food in My house,
And try Me now in this,"
Says the LORD of hosts,
"If I will not open for you the windows of heaven
And pour out for you such blessing
That there will not be room enough to receive it.
And I will rebuke the devourer for your sakes,
So that he will not destroy the fruit of your ground,
Nor shall the vine fail to bear fruit for you in the field,"
Says the LORD of hosts;
"And all nations will call you blessed,
For you will be a delightful land,"
Says the LORD of hosts. (Mal. 3:8–12)

God draws a very clear line. Those who fail to give according to His commandment are not blessed—those who do give tithes and offerings *are* blessed.

- *What new insights do you have into this passage from Malachi 3?*

_____

_____

There are those Christians who believe that tithing was only for Old Testament times. Why didn't Jesus teach about tithing? Because the people were already tithing! Tithing was deeply ingrained in the fabric of the society in which Jesus ministered. There was no reason to preach about something the people were already doing. In fact, the deeply religious Pharisees were tithing the herbs that grew in their gardens. Jesus did not criticize their tithing; instead, He approved of their tithing and said they were to place greater importance on bigger issues: God's justice and God's love. He said, "You tithe mint and rue and all manner of herbs, and pass by justice and the love of God. These you ought to have done, without leaving the others undone" (Luke 11:42).

Jesus also taught a great deal about giving to the needy (see Matt. 25:37–40), and He taught sacrificial giving (Mark 12:41–44).

• *How do you feel when you hear the word* tithe?

_____

_____

• *In what ways are you feeling challenged in your spirit?*

_____

_____

What the Word Says	What the Word Says to Me
All the tithe of the land, whether of the seed of the land or of the fruit of the tree, is the LORD's. It is holy to the LORD . . . And concerning the tithe of the herd or the flock, of whatever passes under the rod, the tenth one shall be holy to the LORD. (Lev. 27:30, 32)	....

Honor the LORD with your pos-
sessions,

And with the firstfruits of all your
increase;

So your barns will be filled with
plenty,

And your vats will overflow with
new wine. (Prov. 3:9–10)

....

....

....

....

....

....

Let us not grow weary while
doing good, for in due season we
shall reap if we do not lose heart.
(Gal. 6:9)

....

....

....

....

3. Generous Giving

We are to be generous givers.

The first-century Christians were generous givers. They not only tithed to the storehouse of the Lord, but in some cases, they sacrificed all they had for the benefit of their brothers and sisters in Christ (see Acts 4:34–37).

The apostle Paul described a ministry gift of giving, and admonished those with this gift to give "with liberality" (Rom. 12:8). Those who are called to such a ministry go beyond the giving of tithes and offerings. All of us, however, are challenged to give with generosity—to go above and beyond the tithe and to give generous offerings.

The degree to which we give is the degree to which we receive.

What the Word Says

Do not be deceived, God is
not mocked; for whatever a man

What the Word Says to Me

....

....

sows, that he will also reap. (Gal. 6:7)

He who sows sparingly will also reap sparingly, and he who sows bountifully will also reap bountifully. (2 Cor. 9:6)

An Expression of Trust in God

Our giving is a direct expression of our trust in God. It is a sign of our willingness to "let go" of the controls of our life and our material well-being and "let God" direct us, use us, and bless us as He desires. The psalmist wrote,

Oh, taste and see that the LORD is good;
Blessed is the man who trusts in Him!
Oh, fear the LORD, you His saints!
There is no want to those who fear Him.
The young lions lack and suffer hunger;
But those who seek the LORD shall not lack any good thing.

(Ps. 34:8–10)

The promise of God to you as His beloved child is that He "shall supply all your need according to His riches in glory by Christ Jesus" (Phil. 4:19).

Are you willing to trust God today with your giving? Are you willing to trust Him to take care of you and to meet all of your material needs?

It takes discipline of your will to become a cheerful, consistent, and generous giver. Your giving is a key, however, to releasing the blessings of God into your life. It is vitally linked to your ability to trust God, and therefore, to your ability to grow spiritually.

• *What new insights do you have into the relationship between giving and spiritual growth?*

_____

_____

• *In what ways are you feeling challenged in your spirit?*

_____

_____

LESSON 8

INVOLVEMENT WITH OTHER BELIEVERS

One of the most important spiritual disciplines you can develop in your life is faithful involvement with other believers. I am always amazed when a Christian tells me, "Oh, I don't go to church very often. I'd rather stay at home and listen to Christian television or radio programs, or listen to Bible-teaching tapes." Others reluctantly admit to me, "We only go to church when we can work it into our family schedule" or "I go to church *as often as I can,*" which usually means not very often. While I certainly am all in favor of Christian television, radio, and tape ministries, I also know they are no substitute for your regular attendance and faithful involvement in the worship services, ministry outreaches, and educational programs of your church.

The writer to the Hebrews said,

Let us consider one another in order to stir up love and good works, not forsaking the assembling of ourselves together, as is the manner of some, but exhorting one another, and so much the more as you see the Day approaching. (Heb. 10:24–25)

• *What insights do you have into this passage from Hebrews?*

_____

_____

The Body of Christ

No Christian has ever been called to "go it alone" in his or her faith walk. We need one another. The church was designed from the beginning to function as the living body of Christ on the earth after the Lord's resurrection and ascension.

The apostle Paul wrote,

> For as we have many members in one body, but all the members do not have the same function, so we, being many, are one body in Christ, and individually members of one another. Having then gifts differing according to the grace that is given to us, let us use them: if prophecy, let us prophesy in proportion to our faith; or ministry, let us use it in our ministering; he who teaches, in teaching; he who exhorts, in exhortation; he who gives, with liberality; he who leads, with diligence; he who shows mercy, with cheerfulness. (Rom. 12:4–8)

Part of the reason we need to be in regular fellowship with other believers is so we might *receive* the benefit of their spiritual gifts, and in turn, *give* our spiritual gifts to the body of Christ. We individually are made stronger as we both receive and give. Simultaneously, the church to which we belong is made stronger and more effective as a whole.

What the Word Says

The bread which we break, is it not the communion of the body of Christ? For we, though many, are one bread and one body; for we all partake of that one bread. (1 Cor. 10:16–17)

And He put all things under His feet, and gave Him to be head over all things to the church, which is His body, the fullness of Him who fills all in all. (Eph. 1:22–23)

For as the body is one and has many members, but all the members of that one body, being many, are one body, so also is Christ. For by one Spirit we were all baptized into one body— whether Jews or Greeks, whether slaves or free—and have all been made to drink into one Spirit. For in fact the body is not one member but many. (1 Cor. 12:12–14)

God has set the members, each one of them, in the body just as He pleased. (1 Cor. 12:18)

What the Word Says to Me

God composed the body, having
given greater honor to that part
which lacks it, that there should
be no schism in the body, but
that the members should have
the same care for one another.
And if one member suffers, all
the members suffer with it; or if
one member is honored, all the
members rejoice with it. (1 Cor.
12:24–26)

- *How do you feel about being a member of the body of Christ?
Do you have both positive and negative feelings? Do you
know why you feel the way you do?*

- *In what ways are you feeling challenged in your spirit?*

Our Ministry to Other Believers

Jesus made it very clear that our foremost ministry to other
believers is to love them. He said to His disciples shortly before
His crucifixion: "This is My commandment, that you love one
another as I have loved you" (John 15:12). The apostle Paul
echoed this command in his writing to the Ephesians: "Be
imitators of God as dear children. And walk in love, as Christ
also has loved us and given Himself for us" (Eph. 5:1–2).

The New Testament writers identified several specific ways
in which we are called to show love to one another within the
body of Christ. Paul wrote to the Colossians,

Let the peace of God rule in your hearts, to which also you were called in one body; and be thankful. Let the word of Christ dwell in you richly in all wisdom, teaching and admonishing one another in psalms and hymns and spiritual songs, singing with grace in your hearts to the Lord. And whatever you do in word or deed, do all in the name of the Lord Jesus, giving thanks to God the Father through Him. (Col. 3:15–17)

As members of the Body of Christ, we are to

- pray for one another (James 5:16).
- speak well of one another (James 4:11).
- speak truthful and admonishing words to one another (Rom. 15:14).
- be hospitable and giving to one another (1 Peter 4:9–10).
- comfort and build up one another (1 Thess. 5:11).
- pursue the common good (1 Thess. 5:15).
- encourage and build up one another (1 Cor. 14:26).
- bless one another (1 Peter 3:8–9).

How much we miss if we isolate ourselves from the body of Christ!

What the Word Says	What the Word Says to Me
Confess your trespasses to one another, and pray for one another, that you may be healed. (James 5:16)	....
Do not speak evil of one another, brethren . . . Who are you to judge another? (James 4:11–12)	....

You also are full of goodness,
filled with all knowledge, able
also to admonish one another.
(Rom. 15:14)

Be hospitable to one another
without grumbling. As each one
has received a gift, minister it to
one another, as good stewards of
the manifold grace of God. (1
Peter 4:9–10)

Comfort each other and edify one
another. (1 Thess. 5:11)

See that no one renders evil for
evil to anyone, but always pursue
what is good both for yourselves
and for all. (1 Thess. 5:15)

How is it then, brethren?
Whenever you come together,
each of you has a psalm, has a
teaching, has a tongue, has a revelation, has an interpretation. Let
all things be done for edification.
(1 Cor. 14:26)

Finally, all of you be of one mind,
having compassion for one
another; love as brothers, be tenderhearted, be courteous; not

returning evil for evil or reviling
for reviling, but on the contrary
blessing, knowing that you were
called to this, that you may
inherit a blessing. (1 Peter 3:8–9)

- *In what specific ways have you been blessed through the years by others in the body of Christ?*

- *In what ways are you feeling challenged in your spirit today?*

Our Service to Others Outside the Church

Along with others in the body of Christ, we are to be involved in active ministry to those who do not know the Lord. Jesus sent out His disciples two by two. He gave them power and authority over all demons, and power to cure diseases. He told them to preach the kingdom of God and heal the sick (Luke 9:1–2).

On another occasion, Jesus sent out seventy of His disciples, again two by two, and He said to them, "The harvest truly is great, but the laborers are few; therefore pray the Lord of the harvest to send out laborers into His harvest . . . Heal the sick there, and say to them, 'The kingdom of God has come near to you'" (Luke 10:2, 9).

If we desire to be followers of Jesus today, we must acknowledge that He is sending us out as well, and He is saying the same things to us—we are to heal the sick and proclaim the kingdom of God.

• *What new insights do you have into these passages from Luke?*

_____

_____

Taking On the Ministry of Christ

Jesus used the words of Isaiah to describe His ministry on earth:

> The Spirit of the Lord GOD is upon Me,
> Because the LORD has anointed Me
> To preach good tidings to the poor;
> He has sent Me to heal the brokenhearted,
> To proclaim liberty to the captives,
> And the opening of the prison to those who are bound;
> To proclaim the acceptable year of the LORD,
> And the day of vengeance of our God;
> To comfort all who mourn,
> To console those who mourn in Zion,
> To give them beauty for ashes,
> The oil of joy for mourning,
> The garment of praise for the spirit of heaviness;
> That they may be called trees of righteousness,
> The planting of the LORD, that He may be glorified. (Isa. 61:1–3)

If we are truly to be the body of *Christ* on the earth today, shouldn't we be engaged in these very same ministries?

• *What insights do you have into this passage from Isaiah 61 as these verses apply to your life and the life of your church?*

_____

_____

Jesus also taught His disciples,

> Then the King will say to those on His right hand, "Come, you blessed of My Father, inherit the kingdom prepared for you from the foundation of the world: for I was hungry and you gave Me food; I was thirsty and you gave Me drink; I was a stranger and you took Me in; I was naked and you clothed Me; I was sick and you visited Me; I was in prison and you came to Me." Then the righteous will answer Him, saying, "Lord, when did we see You hungry and feed You, or thirsty and give You drink? When did we see You a stranger and take You in, or naked and clothe You? Or when did we see You sick, or in prison, and come to You?" And the King will answer and say to them, "Assuredly, I say to you, inasmuch as you did it to one of the least of these My brethren, you did it to Me." (Matt. 25:34–40)

• *What insights do you have into this passage from Matthew 25?*

_____

_____

Just as we are never called to "go it alone" in our faith walk, we are never called to "go it alone" in ministry to others. Jesus sent out His disciples *two by two*. He said about our ministry, "If two of you agree on earth concerning anything that they ask, it will be done for them by My Father in heaven. For where two or three are gathered together in My name, I am there in the midst of them" (Matt. 18:19–20).

Paul encouraged the Philippians, "Stand fast in one spirit, with one mind striving together for the faith of the gospel" (Phil. 1:27).

In Revelation, John recorded again and again these four convicting words of Jesus that He spoke to the churches: "I know your works" (see Rev. 2:2, 9, 19 as examples). What we do as the body of Christ—as unto the Lord, unto one another, and unto the lost—is the basis on which we will be judged and rewarded.

- *What new insights do you have into the importance of ministry —both to the body of Christ and as the body of Christ—in developing spiritual strength?*

  _____

  _____

- *In what ways are you feeling challenged in your spirit?*

  _____

  _____

LESSON 9

THE FOUR R'S OF SPIRITUAL GROWTH

Are you aware that Christians are *commanded* to grow spiritually? We are commanded to practice spiritual disciplines and to mature. Peter said, "Grow in the grace and knowledge of our Lord and Savior Jesus Christ" (2 Peter 3:18). This is not a nice statement of encouragement or advice—it is an "order" from the Lord.

None of us automatically grow spiritually. We each must choose to grow. And, we must choose to *continue* to grow. We must never be satisfied with our current level of spiritual strength. We must always seek to become stronger, more mature, and more effective for the Lord.

In God's Word, we find four keys that are prerequisites to growth, no matter how mature a person may be in the Lord.

1. Ready to Face Failures

Most of us try to dismiss, sidestep, or justify our faults and failures. We sometimes try to take the easy way out, saying, "That's just the way I am" or "That's the way I was raised." The fact is, most of us are not "just the way God wants us to be." Before the basic spiritual disciplines can be truly effective in causing us to mature into the likeness of Christ Jesus, we must face our faults and failures, take responsibility for them, and go to God with them.

Is there an area in your life where you have experienced repeated failures? Can you point to certain faults that you seem to have had all your life? Let me assure you, God has a way for those failures to be turned into victories and those faults to be turned into strengths. God has a great desire to see you made whole, and He will continue to pursue the faults and failures that fragment you and cause you to be dysfunctional, uneasy, or deeply frustrated. He will continue to move against any obstacle or barrier that stands in the way of your experiencing wholeness or intimacy with Him.

The first step is one we must take: Own up to our failures, flaws, and faults. Stop blaming others and assume responsibility. Confess to God, "I have brought myself to the place where I am today." Admit, "I am the one who has allowed this past to continue to be my present."

True repentance is moving in the opposite direction of past sin. It is an act of the will, empowered by the Holy Spirit within us, to change from our wicked ways, evil attitudes, hurtful words, and wrong behaviors. For a person truly to repent, he first must own up to those things that need to be changed.

If the spiritual disciplines you practice are going to be effective, you must recognize that some things about your life need healing, and that you are responsible for using your will and faith to bring about changes.

- *How do you feel about changing those things in your life that you know are contrary to God's desire for you?*

_____

_____

What the Word Says	What the Word Says to Me
Therefore we also, since we are surrounded by so great a cloud of witnesses, let us lay aside every weight, and the sin which so easily ensnares us, and let us run with endurance the race that is set before us. (Heb. 12:1)	....
Do not grieve the Holy Spirit of God, by whom you were sealed for the day of redemption. Let all bitterness, wrath, anger, clamor, and evil speaking be put away from you, with all malice. And be kind to one another, tender-hearted, forgiving one another, even as God in Christ forgave you. (Eph. 4:30–32)	....
Thus says the Lord GOD: "Repent, turn away from your idols, and turn your faces away from all your abominations." (Ezek. 14:6)	....

2. Receive Godly Counsel

Every Christian, no matter his degree of spiritual strength and maturity, can benefit from wise counsel that is couched in love, forgiveness, and confidentiality. God has placed Christian brothers and sisters in your life to encourage you, to admonish you, to teach you, and to give you godly counsel regarding

God's unique plan and purpose for your life. Avail yourself of their help!

In order to benefit from wise counsel, a person must choose to be transparent and vulnerable emotionally. He must choose to be candid, forthcoming, and truthful about his own life, desires, and motivations. He must face up to the fact that he does not know *fully* all that God desires for him to know, and that he needs the greater wisdom that can come only as we *share* our life in Christ.

Always, the Word of God is the basis for wise counsel. All advice that we receive must flow from God's Word and be echoed by God's Word.

If you truly desire to grow to full spiritual maturity in Christ Jesus, you need to avail yourself of the wisdom that others can offer to you.

 • *In reflecting on your Christian walk, can you cite specific ways in which you have benefited from wise spiritual counselors, teachers, and mentors in the faith?*

What the Word Says

[Jesus taught,] "I still have many things to say to you, but you cannot bear them now. However, when He, the Spirit of truth, has come, He will guide you into all truth; for He will not speak on His own authority, but whatever He hears He will speak; and He will tell you things to come. He

What the Word Says to Me

....

....

....

....

....

....

....

....

will glorify Me, for He will take of ....
what is Mine and declare it to ....
you." (John 16:12–14) ....

My beloved brethren, let every ....
man be swift to hear. (James ....
1:19) ....

3. Reflect on God's Work

The Bible commands us to live a *daily* life—to trust God to meet our daily needs and to walk fully in the present moment of our existence. At the same time, we find numerous instances in God's Word in which the people were called to reflect upon God's goodness to them, or to catch a glimpse of the broader, universal, and eternal work that God is doing—both in the world as a whole today, and throughout the ages.

It is as we learn about and study the ways in which God has worked in the lives of others—not only the people we read about in the Bible but in the course of history—that we gain a greater understanding of how God will work in our lives. We can learn a great deal by hearing and reflecting upon the way God is working in the lives of other Christians today, including those whom we recognize as being more mature in Christ Jesus.

If you are to benefit fully from practicing spiritual disciplines, you need to be able to see your life in the broader context of what God is doing in the world . . . and what He *desires* to do. You must see how your life meshes with the lives of others in your family, your church, and your community. You must gain an understanding that what the Lord desires to do in you is aimed at what the Lord desires ultimately to do *through* you.

- *In your experience with Christ Jesus, how have you benefited from the examples of other Christians, both in history and in your own life?*

_____

_____

What the Word Says

Now, therefore, you are no longer strangers and foreigners, but fellow citizens with the saints and members of the household of God, having been built on the foundation of the apostles and prophets, Jesus Christ Himself being the chief cornerstone, in whom the whole building, being fitted together, grows into a holy temple in the Lord, in whom you also are being built together for a dwelling place of God in the Spirit. (Eph. 2:19–22)

There is one body and one Spirit, just as you were called in one hope of your calling; one Lord, one faith, one baptism; one God and Father of all, who is above all, and through all, and in you all. But to each one of us grace was given according to the measure of Christ's gift. (Eph. 4:4–7)

What the Word Says to Me

_____

4. Response to Trials

The person who practices spiritual disciplines and is growing in Christ Jesus must recognize that he is going to face trials and tests in life. Many people believe that God can and should spare a Christian from all negative experiences. In fact, God *uses* trials and tests for our benefit. They become our opportunity to learn more about God's methods, purposes, and perfect plan—they are our "school" for learning how to grow stronger in faith.

If you are practicing spiritual disciplines, you are going to be better equipped to face trials and tests that come your way. Rather than run from them, or deny their existence, ask the Lord why He has allowed a specific trial or test to come into your life. Look for the lesson He desires to teach you or the character trait He desires to strengthen. God knows all about the trial or test you are experiencing, and He has allowed it to come into your life for a purpose. Ask Him to reveal that purpose to you. Ask Him to help you trust Him to bring you through the trial in a way that results in glory to Him.

At the same time, ask the Lord if the trial or trouble you are experiencing is a "chastening" from Him. The Lord only chastens those whom He loves and desires to perfect. Ask the Lord, "Is there something in my life that You desire for me to change?" If the answer is "Yes," act quickly to obey the Lord's directive or to confess the sin that is holding you back from spiritual growth.

• *In reflecting on your Christian walk, can you cite ways in which trials and tests strengthened you spiritually or deepened your relationship with the Lord?*

_____

_____

What the Word Says	What the Word Says to Me
Beloved, do not think it strange concerning the fiery trial which is to try you, as though some strange thing happened to you; but rejoice to the extent that you partake of Christ's sufferings, that when His glory is revealed, you may also be glad with exceeding joy . . . If anyone suffers as a Christian, let him not be ashamed, but let him glorify God in this matter. (1 Peter 4:12–13, 16)	
"My son, do not despise the chastening of the LORD, Nor be discouraged when you are rebuked by Him; For whom the LORD loves He chastens, And scourges every son whom He receives . . ." We have had human fathers who corrected us, and we paid them respect. Shall we not much more readily be in subjection to the Father of spirits and live? For they indeed for a few days chastened us as seemed best to them but He for our profit, that we may be partakers of His holiness. (Heb. 12:5–6, 9–10)	

We must never lose sight of the fact that we are in relationship with a *holy* God. God manifests no darkness, no shadow of turning, and no tolerance for evil or deceit. For us to approach God, we must be in a state of forgiveness, which is only made possible as we face up to our sin, seek God's forgiveness, and choose to live in His righteousness. This is a daily decision we each must make: a daily decision to confess our sin, a daily receiving of His forgiveness, and a daily desire to walk in the paths the Holy Spirit reveals to us.

Can a person who refuses to face his failures and faults grow spiritually? No.

Can a person who refuses to receive godly counsel truly grow into great spiritual maturity? No.

Can a person who does not see his life in the broader context of God's plan for all mankind truly know how to *employ* spiritual strength and power? No.

Can a person who is unwilling to face life's trials and troubles with a reliance upon God become strong spiritually? No.

Can a person who is unwilling to be chastened by the Lord grow into perfection in Christ Jesus? No.

We each must be willing to face our faults, confess our sins, receive godly counsel, seek God's "big picture" for our life, trust God regardless of circumstances, and yield to the chastening of the Lord if we are to benefit fully from the practice of spiritual disciplines.

A Christian can read his Bible daily, communicate with the Lord often in prayer, attend church regularly, be involved in outreach ministry, and give faithfully, but unless he is willing to change, to grow, to be perfected, and then to be used however and whenever and wherever God desires, these disciplines will not yield their maximum benefit.

A total submission of our life to God's remolding and remaking of us is required.

- *What new insights do you have into the process of spiritual growth?*

  _____

  _____

- *In what ways are you feeling challenged in your spirit today?*

  _____

  _____

TEN HALLMARKS OF SPIRITUAL STRENGTH

How will you know when you are spiritually strong and mature in Christ Jesus? What is the result for those who diligently practice spiritual disciplines and seek to grow spiritually?

From my many years of pastoring, I have concluded that there are ten hallmarks or "signs" that routinely appear in those who are spiritually strong. As you read through these attributes and study them, I encourage you to evaluate your own life . . . and to refrain from judging others. Not all of these attributes may be present in a person with equal strength, but these are the marks of a person who is spiritually healthy and mature. They are the attributes of a person who has grown to a deep level of intimacy with God and who routinely experiences God's presence and power in his life.

1. A Great Hunger for God

Those who are spiritually mature have a hunger for the things of God. This hunger is what has led them to develop spiritual disciplines and to mature in Christ Jesus. Those with a hunger for God are not content with knowing Him in an objective way as Creator, Savior, or almighty God. They desire to know Him as Lord—to develop an intimate relationship with the Lord, to know what the Lord desires of them and for them, and to experience the Lord's presence on a daily basis. They want to know God in all His fullness—Father, Son, and Holy Spirit. They desire to recognize and respond immediately to the prompting of the Holy Spirit, however He may lead them.

- *Do you have a "hunger" for God in your life? Do you continue to desire to know Him better?*

_____

_____

What the Word Says

As the deer pants for the water brooks,
So pants my soul for You, O God.
My soul thirsts for God, for the living God. (Ps. 42:1–2)

What things were gain to me, these things I have counted loss for Christ. Yet indeed I also count all things loss for the excellence of the knowledge of Christ Jesus my Lord . . . that I may gain Christ and be found in Him. (Phil. 3:7–9)

What the Word Says to Me

----

2. A Desire to Know God's Truth

The spiritually mature person knows God's Word and continually seeks to apply it in his life. He not only knows what the Bible has to say, but he also knows the meaning of the Scriptures and considers God's Word to be the ultimate authority in helping him make decisions and eternally significant choices.

- *How do you feel about knowing God's truth? Is it a top priority in your life?*

_____

_____

What the Word Says	What the Word Says to Me
In His word I do hope. (Ps. 130:5)	
Teach me, O LORD, the way of Your statutes, And I shall keep it to the end. Give me understanding, and I shall keep Your law; Indeed, I shall observe it with my whole heart. (Ps. 119:33–34)	

3. No Tolerance for Evil

The spiritually mature person has no tolerance for evil in any form. He is able to discern evil, recognize sin, and has an abhorrence for all that is contrary to God's goodness, grace, mercy, love, and forgiveness.

This does not mean that the spiritually mature Christian is judgmental of people, but rather, of actions and words. Christians are called to judge *deeds*—to judge right from wrong (see 1 Peter 4:17). The mature Christian has a desire to remove himself as far as possible from activities and situations that give rise to sin.

- *As you look back over your life, can you cite things that once attracted you that you no longer find attractive or worthy of your time, energy, or finances?*

_____

_____

What the Word Says

Beloved, do not believe every spirit, but test the spirits, whether they are of God; because many false prophets have gone out into the world. By this you know the Spirit of God: Every spirit that confesses that Jesus Christ has come in the flesh is of God, and every spirit that does not confess that Jesus Christ has come in the flesh is not of God. (1 John 4:1–3)

His divine power has given to us all things that pertain to life and godliness, through the knowledge of Him who called us by glory and virtue. (2 Peter 1:3)

What the Word Says to Me

_____

_____

_____

_____

_____

_____

_____

_____

_____

_____

_____

_____

_____

_____

_____

Turn away my eyes from looking ....
at worthless things, And revive ....
me in Your way. (Ps. 119:37) ....

4. A Desire for God's Will to Be Done

The Bible teaches that we as believers are *in* this world, but we are not to be *of* this world. As believers in the world, we must abide by natural laws, live within the constraints of man-made laws, and provide for ourselves within the "systems" of this world. But we are not to have the same desires and lusts that the world exhibits. We are not to have the same dreams, goals, or hopes. Rather, we are to desire with our whole hearts that God's will be done on this earth. As we pray in the Lord's Prayer, "Thy kingdom come. Thy will be done in earth, as it is in heaven" (Matt. 6:10 KJV).

• *Do you have a strong desire to live your life GOD's way?*

_____

_____

What the Word Says	**What the Word Says to Me**
Set your mind on things above, not on things on the earth. (Col. 3:2)	....
Now we have received, not the spirit of the world, but the Spirit who is from God, that we might know the things that have been freely given to us by God. (1 Cor. 2:12)	....

Do not love the world or the things in the world. If anyone loves the world, the love of the Father is not in him . . . And the world is passing away, and the lust of it; but he who does the will of God abides forever. (1 John 2:15–17)

5. A Growing Love for Others

The spiritually strong person not only exhibits spiritual power, but also great love. The mature Christian is able to express love and has a desire to extend love to an ever-widening circle of people. The mature Christian has little concern with appearances, status, or personal reputation. His foremost concern is with expressing God's love to the sinner and to any person in need. He has an ever-growing desire to reach out, to touch, to speak, to share, to listen, and to be used by God to shower His love on those who are hurting.

• *In your Christian walk, can you cite specific ways in which your ability to love has increased or your willingness to express love has grown?*

What the Word Says

If someone says, "I love God," and hates his brother, he is a liar; for he who does not love his brother whom he has seen, how can he love God whom he has not

What the Word Says to Me

seen? And this commandment we have from Him; that he who loves God must love his brother also. (1 John 4:20–21)

[Jesus taught,] "'You shall love the LORD your God with all your heart, with all your soul, and with all your mind.' This is the first and great commandment. And the second is like it: 'You shall love your neighbor as yourself.'" (Matt. 22:37–39)

6. Quickness to Forgive

The spiritually strong person is quick to forgive those who offend, wrong, hurt, or reject him. He harbors no resentment and is quick to make apologies, seek to make amends, and settle disputes peacefully. Does he compromise with evil or have a greater desire to be yoked with nonbelievers? No! The mature Christian, rather, has a desire to live in peace with others and to live free of bitterness and feelings of revenge.

• *How do you feel when others hurt you or reject you?*

What the Word Says

[Jesus taught,] "Love your enemies, do good, and lend, hoping for nothing in return; and your reward will be great, and

What the Word Says to Me

you will be sons of the Most
High. For He is kind to the
unthankful and evil. Therefore be
merciful, just as your Father also
is merciful. Judge not, and you
shall not be judged. Condemn
not, and you shall not be con-
demned. Forgive, and you will be
forgiven." (Luke 6:35–37)

7. Quickness to Obey

When the spiritually mature person receives a directive
from the Holy Spirit, he is quick to act. When he feels a conviction of sin, he is quick to confess his sin, seek God's forgiveness, and change his ways. The mature Christian has a deep
desire to do God's will. He longs to hear God speak to him, and
when He does, he responds enthusiastically and immediately,
with full effort given to whatever God commands.

• *In looking back over your Christian walk, can you see that
you are now quicker to say yes to God?*

What the Word Says

Now it shall come to pass, if you
diligently obey the voice of the
LORD your God, to observe care-
fully all His commandments
which I command you today, that
the LORD your God will set you

What the Word Says to Me

high above all nations of the
earth. And all these blessings
shall come upon you and over-
take you, because you obey the
voice of the LORD your God.
(Deut. 28:1–2)

[Jesus said,] "Whoever hears
these sayings of Mine, and does
them, I will liken him to a wise
man who built his house on the
rock: and the rain descended, the
floods came, and the winds blew
and beat on that house; and it did
not fall, for it was founded on the
rock." (Matt. 7:24–25)

8. Great Faith

Every person has been given a measure of faith (Rom.
12:3). But not every believer has developed the same degree of
faith. Faith is intended to be used, to be exercised. And the
more a person uses his faith, the stronger it grows. The Bible
speaks of varying degrees of faith—from "little faith" (see
Matt. 14:31), to "great faith" (see Matt. 15:28). The mature
believer is a person who is developing and using his faith with
the goal of having *great* faith.

• *Can you look back on your Christian life and see that your
faith has grown?*

What the Word Says	What the Word Says to Me
For in it [the gospel of Christ] the righteousness of God is revealed from faith to faith; as it is written, "The just shall live by faith." (Rom. 1:17)	----------------------------------
	----------------------------------

We are bound to thank God always for you, brethren, as it is fitting, because your faith grows exceedingly. (2 Thess. 1:3)	----------------------------------
	----------------------------------

	----------------------------------

9. A Soft Heart

The spiritually strong person has a soft heart toward those in need—he is tender and sensitive to those who are hurting, and he desires to respond in ways that are appropriate and bring glory to God. He has a strong desire to see sinners receive Jesus Christ as their Savior. He has a commitment to help in whatever way he can to see that the practical, emotional, and spiritual needs of others are met.

• *How do you feel toward those who are in need?*

What the Word Says	What the Word Says to Me
Be kindly affectionate to one another with brotherly love, in honor giving preference to one another; not lagging in diligence,	----------------------------------

fervent in spirit, serving the Lord;
rejoicing in hope, patient in tribulation, continuing steadfastly in
prayer; distributing to the needs
of the saints, given to hospitality.
(Rom. 12:10–13)

Rejoice with those who rejoice,
and weep with those who weep.
(Rom. 12:15)

10. Deep Love for God

The spiritually mature person has a deep and abiding love
for God. He recognizes God as his loving, merciful, tender,
patient heavenly Father—a Father who can be trusted completely to provide, give wisdom, be present always, bestow
blessings, and give unconditional love.

• *As you reflect upon your Christian walk, can you see how
your feelings of love have grown toward God?*

What the Word Says	What the Word Says to Me
The love of God has been poured out in our hearts by the Holy Spirit who was given to us. (Rom. 5:5)	
We love Him because He first loved us. (1 John 4:19)	

Are you satisfied today with your level of spiritual maturity? Are you the person you desire to be when you see Jesus face-to-face? If not, ask the Lord to help you develop a hunger to know Him better and to show you how you might grow in your spirit.

- *What new insights do you have into the life that is manifested by those who routinely practice spiritual disciplines over time?*

  _____

  _____

- *In what ways are you feeling challenged in your spirit?*

  _____

  _____

CONCLUSION

THE BASICS NEVER CHANGE

Every coach knows that when a team gets into trouble, that is not the time to introduce new plays or change the overall strategy. Rather, it's time to "return to basics," to reinforce the tried-and-true drills and practices.

The same is true spiritually. Down through the ages, Christians have known that when they practice basic spiritual disciplines—reading God's Word daily, praying often, giving faithfully, attending church regularly, staying active in outreach ministries—they are much more likely to

- hear from God.
- experience God's love, joy, and peace.
- grow in the effective use of their talents.
- receive blessings beyond anything they had asked or imagined (see Eph. 3:20).

We never grow beyond our need for the basics. They are the foundation on which all other aspects of our Christian life are built. They are the disciplines that need to become deeply ingrained habits in us.

In which area of spiritual discipline do you find yourself lacking?

Make the developing or renewal of that particular discipline a priority in your life, without neglecting the other disciplines. And then see what God will do in you, through you, and for you. It is as we practice the basics—regularly, consistently, and with perseverance—that we grow and become strong in the Lord.